PRIMARY SCHOOL CONFIDENTIAL

Mrs Woog is a mouthy forty-something housewife from the burbs. She writes the popular blog WoogsWorld, which is about all kinds of things but mainly what is going on in her head. She covers family, politics, food, travel, some very lame attempts at fashion, social issues, wine, cheese. And laundry. She is pretty much running late all the time, and will more often or not turn up somewhere with food spilt down her top. Mrs Woog is married to Mr Woog, and they have two gorgeous yet lively sons. In a former life Mrs Woog was a primary school teacher.

Visit Mrs Woog's blog @ woogsworld.com.

BY
MRS WOOG

PRIMARY SCHOOL CONFIDENTIAL

ALLEN&UNWIN
SYDNEY•MELBOURNE•AUCKLAND•LONDON

Certain names and details have been changed to protect the innocent and guilty alike.

First published in 2016

Copyright © Kayte Murphy 2016

Allen & Unwin
83 Alexander Street
Crows Nest NSW 2065
Australia
Phone: (61 2) 8425 0100
Email: info@allenandunwin.com
Web: www.allenandunwin.com

Cataloguing-in-Publication details are available
from the National Library of Australia
www.trove.nla.gov.au

ISBN 978 1 76011 373 5

Set in 11.25/17.25 pt Sabon LT Pro by Bookhouse
Printed and bound in Australia by Griffin Press

10 9 8 7 6 5 4 3 2 1

MIX
Paper from
responsible sources
FSC® C009448
www.fsc.org

The paper in this book is FSC® certified.
FSC® promotes environmentally responsible,
socially beneficial and economically viable
management of the world's forests.

For John

CONTENTS

—INTRODUCTION—

SHE WHO CANNOT, BLOGS

My name is Mrs Woog and I am a mummy blogger. I know this because I have two sons and I write on the internet. Originally known as a 'mommy' blogger, we first became an acknowledged genre of writing back in the early 2000s in the United States, where bored moms began personal websites, or weblogs as they were originally called, to connect with others in the same boat (that being a boat often full of tediousness and monotony, which can come along when you are drowning in small children). All of a sudden there was someone out there listening, nodding along and offering advice. Communities were formed and continue to grow to this day.

In 2008 a well-meaning friend suggested I start my own blog. I couldn't see any reason not to, so that year I opened a blogspot account and typed in the title WOOGSWORLD. It was a nod to my husband's unusual Hungarian surname, and a nod to the brilliant and classic 1992 film *Wayne's World*.

Armed with very little enthusiasm, I wrote six posts that year. I selected the moniker Mrs Woog because, at the time, I wanted to remain anonymous on the internet.* (And I believed that the chance anyone would read this mummy blog was very remote.)

The year 2009 was very quiet for my blog: I wrote one post. It was about my neighbours, who I suspected were swingers. You see, I was beginning to go quite stir crazy, and cabin fevery, and was desperate for adult social intercourse. I began talking a lot to religious folk who knocked on my door. When the two boys were down for their naps, I had forty-five minute conversations with Indian call-centre workers who would phone to sell me stuff.

Then something happened. Something that would go on to change the course of my career. Something that would prevent me from thinking about opening a bottle of wine at 11 am ever, ever again.

I was up at the local Blockbuster and rented a film called *Julie & Julia*. It was the true story of Julie Powell, who had also dug herself into a deep rut. Inspired by food and the work of famed cook Julia Child, she vowed to blog through Child's cookbook *Mastering the Art of French Cooking*.

T'was like a fire had been lit in my belly. Of course! I would resurrect my blog and write a story on it every single day for a year. But what would I write about? I wasn't doing anything particularly inspiring. I mean, a night down at the local beer garden with a pram and the old ball and chain was okay, but it certainly wasn't going to be riveting reading. So I decided just to write what was in front of me. I added a tagline 'Making the most out of the mundane', and dutifully wrote a piece every

---

* If you think you can remain anonymous on the internet, you are dreaming.

day. But at the end of the year, much like Forrest Gump, I just kept going.

It's a funny way to find your real passion and your true calling. I ended up just where I needed to be: I am a writer. In the chapters that follow you will see how I needed to go through the other chapters of my life, before I could get to the start of this one.

She who cannot, blogs. And that is just fine by me.

But I am not only a blogger, I am also a former primary school teacher.

I finished high school in 1991, and to say that I was a disappointment to my parents is putting it very, very lightly. I had spent the last two years of school trying to avoid going. I was a disgrace to the establishment, as will become clear through the chapters of this book.

The day the HSC results arrived—in the old fashioned way, via Australia Post—I stood in the dining room in front of my parents, whose faces were flushed with excitement. They had paid a lot of money for my world-class education and were expecting great things. My older sister had performed brilliantly (and, later, my younger siblings would all do very well indeed).

But I could not share in their enthusiasm, as I was quite aware that the envelope was not going contain wonderful news. Under their expectant gaze, I opened my results to reveal . . .

57.9

Those three little digits were to change the course of my life.

Earlier in the year, I had applied to Charles Sturt University to study journalism, as writing was my first love. My entrance essay, I was told, showed a lot of promise. But my dream of being the modern-day Dorothy Parker vanished as quickly as my parents' smiles.

I excused myself from the dining room to let them digest this news. Meanwhile, I rang my boyfriend Peter to tell him I was in some pretty deep shit. It turned out he was in some pretty deep shit of his own; his tone veering between fury and disbelief, he informed me that he had been awarded the lowest result it was possible to get: the mysterious '15 and under'. This meant he had scored less than 15 per cent, and the Department of Education was not going to humiliate him further by revealing his actual mark.

'There must be some mistake!' he fumed.

I didn't have the heart to tell him that there probably was no mistake, for even I could barely read his illegible writing.

Perhaps if we hadn't spent every waking moment with our tongues shoved down each other's throats, we might both have ended up with more respectable scores. But that's a moot point. Clearly, I was not destined to be a journalist. It was obvious even then that I didn't have the focus and drive required to succeed in such a cutthroat industry.

And so I shall be forever grateful for that 57.9. Had I made the grade, there is a fairly high chance that by now I would be a raging alcoholic editing the obituaries section of the *Daily Liberal* in Dubbo. Not that I mind Dubbo at all. In fact, my oldies owned a pub there when I was young, and I have fond memories of the stench of stale cigarette smoke and the dregs of old KB beer. And, as it happens, my old love Peter—with whom I reconnected many years later—is now enjoying life as the owner of a very popular country pub with his wife and two daughters.

But back to that eighteen-year-old me. What the fuck was I going to do with my life?

It was highly unlikely that I was going to stumble into a young Jamie Packer's arms at the polo, my bosom heaving in a JAG bodysuit and my long blonde hair rippling in the breeze created by the rush of ponies thundering past. Unfortunately I had boofy brown hair that could never be tamed and hips that came in at about the age of twelve, but not in an admirable way.

No. I was going to have to use my brain and not my body to get ahead. The problem was, my brain had not come into its own just yet.

My parents were adamant that their investment in my education was going to have to pay dividends at some point, and that meant university was non-negotiable. So I scrolled through the list of courses that I might possibly be accepted into.

It basically came down to nursing or primary school teaching. Nursing was never a contender, as the mere sight of blood, pus or vomit sets me off on a dry-retching fit that can last for hours. So I ticked the box to become a primary school teacher with as much consideration as one might devote to choosing toilet paper.

And from this inauspicious beginning grew my immersion in the very particular world that is primary school. It's a world that has been more or less overlooked in the canon of child-rearing tomes. There are shelves and shelves of baby books. There are whole volumes devoted to advising new parents when to introduce carrot puree into their baby's diet or how to identify every conceivable rash a baby or toddler might sprout. But where is all the information on raising primary school children?

If you picked up this book thinking it would help you to navigate the wonder years of the infants and primary school playground in any sensible, well-thought-out, heavily researched way, however, I am sorry to tell you that you're going to get a little less—or a lot more—than you bargained for.

I am going to give it to you from every side*: from my own school days to my time as a primary school teacher, having to deal with annoying, well . . . everything . . . to being the parent of primary school kids myself. And I hope that, along the way, you'll pause to recall your own days in the old school yard, to recall your favourite teachers—and to enjoy a frank assessment of the trials and tribulations of the modern parent.

---

* Please note that I am NOT a child psychologist in any way, and this book is chockas full of generalisations. And then some.

—PART ONE—

SCHOOL DAYS, SCHOOL DAYS

—|—

THE KINDY KID

In 1978 our family moved from the country town of Tamworth, where I was born, to a small suburb on the fringes of Sydney. The following year I was to start school at North Richmond Public School and I just could not wait. My older sister having paved the way before me, I felt no fear or apprehension; I was just raring to go.

I chose my own school case. Nowadays school cases would be practically illegal, though I'm sure physios and chiropractors the country over would rub their hands with glee at the thought of all the long-term back and neck injuries they would cause.

These days, school bags are designed with proper attention to posture and spinal care, and there are guidelines to ensure that you don't screw up their purchase. These include:

- Choose a backpack with padded shoulders.
- Make sure weight is distributed evenly.

- The actual weight of a packed backpack should not exceed 10 per cent of the child's overall body weight.
- The bag should sit between the tops of the shoulders and the small of the back.

I mean, is it any wonder the incidence of anxiety is on the increase when something as simple as giving your kid a bag to take to school needs so much careful consideration?

But I had a school case. It was bright yellow, with black corners and a snappy black handle. I loved it so much. It was the size of one of Mum's large Coolabah casks and could fit a Vegemite sandwich and an apple, with room to spare. This was what I was carrying when, clutching Mum's hand, I arrived for my first day of school.

I was assigned to Miss Babos's class and would go on to be a proud member of KB. Miss Babos was what every kindy teacher should be: kind, patient and, to my young eyes, resembling a beauty queen. She had long, shiny blonde hair—and talk about fashionable! Wearing long boots and a gored skirt, topped with a skivvy, she looked like she had just stepped off the set of *The Brady Bunch*. In fact, Miss Babos was the spitting image of Marcia Brady, who was very much a style idol of mine, even at the age of five.

I took to school like a pig to mud. Everything about it was just bloody marvellous, from sitting in little groups, to nap time, to reading in the library at lunchtimes when the days were so hot that the birds fell from the sky. Mum would do canteen duty on occasion, and it was on these days I was the most popular girl in the class, promising icy poles in exchange for six hours of friendship.

4

I'm afraid to say the icy poles were necessary, for I was not one of those cute, appealing kindy kids. I was the FLK—the funny-looking kid—skinny as a stick of dried spaghetti with wispy, nondescript-coloured hair that stuck up in random clumps, Coke-bottle glasses, and teeth that were growing any which way they pleased, which was mainly out.

It was not only my teeth that stood out. During kindergarten my parents separated, and at the time it was quite the novelty to come from a 'broken home'. I was the only kid in my class whose parents did not live under the same roof. This made me different, and I can still recall the sympathetic looks I would get from the ladies in the office, the other teachers and mothers of my friends.

(It was not to remain like this forever. My mum would soon marry a marvellous man, the local solicitor who was recently widowed. A step sister and later a half sister would be added to our family. Just what we needed. More kids.)

But there were other kids who were 'different'. A lot lived in the local housing commission streets, including the notorious (at the time) but inappropriately named Sunnyside Crescent. These were dangerous streets, as students from the local high school would hang around on their bikes, throwing rocks at people who passed by.

We were forbidden ever to go east of Grose Wold Road, unless we were going to Gazza's Northo Takeaway. But a second eatery was established that year, bringing yet another 'different' family to the community. The Mountain Palace opened to much fanfare; it was so exotic and fancy, with red-and-gold flocked wallpaper and real napkins arranged in the shape of fans. The two sons of the proprietors came to my school—and back in 1980 racism was rife. Cries of 'Ching Chong Chinaman' followed them everywhere they went. It was my first exposure to racism, and even then I knew it was wrong.

Another notable thing that happened to me during my kindergarten year was my first encounter with a penis. I had finished up another hard day of identifying colours and operating scissors and, together with my sister, was trotting down Pecks Road towards home. As we passed the local high school, a place where demountable classrooms went to die, we were approached by a teenage boy, who asked whether we would like to see a cocky.

Of course we wanted to see a cocky! Who wouldn't?

So he pulled down his pants and wagged his penis at us.

That was it?! Disappointed, we continued on our way, swinging our spine-damaging cases in the afternoon sun.

Later, over dinner, Mum asked us how our day was.

'This boy said he would show us his bird, but he showed us his willy instead,' I complained.

For some reason this set Mum off. She made a series of furious phone calls, and the next day the young man was formally identified and chastised. We were told that we had to walk home via William Street from now on.

North Richmond was your typical Aussie suburb, a place where your parents would write a note and give you a few bucks, and you could go up to the milk bar and fetch their cigarettes for them. And as in many other typical Aussie suburbs, footy was worshipped far more than any religion. My Western Suburbs Magpies jumper was my most treasured possession. If you had asked me what I wanted to be when I grew up, I would reply, 'Tommy Raudonikis,' with a completely straight face.

No one was concerned about childhood obesity in those days, because it was so rare. Most of the kids were long and lean, growing up on a diet of proper food and plenty of outdoor activities. We were allowed to watch *The Wide World of Disney* each Sunday night for an hour and that was it. The rest of the time, we had to be outside. Even at the age of five, we were told to bugger off and explore. Luckily we lived in a cul-de-sac with a creek bubbling away at the bottom of it, so there was always plenty to do. Unfortunately, many of our chosen pursuits resulted in trips to the local hospital to be stitched up after stepping on smashed glass in the creek or to get your noggin put back together after connecting face first with the bitumen when a bike jump went completely wrong.

Yet despite my tomboy antics and desire to be a professional footballer when I grew up, I still—like so many young girls—coveted pretty costumes and shiny crowns. But I'm afraid my unprepossessing appearance led to my first experience of public humiliation.

It was coming up to the end of the year, and everyone's attention had turned to the nativity play—a Christmas school tradition that has long since died out thanks to the controversy that surrounds religion in schools. Hell, my mum was an atheist, and then a Buddhist, but she didn't give a damn about the fact that I was going to be the head angel, come hell or high water. That was my dream, you see; my goal. Not only did the head angel get the most stage time and the prettiest costume, complete with silver, sparkly wings—she alone got to wear a halo, a magnificent headpiece draped in silver tinsel.

I spent hours in front of the bathroom mirror practising standing still and looking celestial, and just as well I did because the audition process was fairly brutal. To begin with, all those who wanted to play Joseph or Mary were asked to stand. I stayed seated; there was no *way* I wanted to wear the dull brown sack that was Mary's costume. Yuck!

Then everyone who wanted a shot at being the head angel was asked to stand. I leapt up and assumed the position I had been practising so diligently. My still and celestial bearing immediately caught Miss Babos's eye.

She told me to sit down.

It turned out the decision had already been made, and Natalie Brown took the crown (well, halo). Natalie Brown, with her big blue eyes and tiny physique. She had the sort of curly, white-blonde hair that would be an American kiddie-pageant stage mom's dream come true. I vowed to hate Natalie Brown for the rest of my life.

Later, at home, I wept big tears into my mother's bosom. She soothed me with her kind words, assuring me that one day I would grow up to become Miss Australia. This title was a very big deal back in 1979, and was used as a yardstick for women who desired to achieve great things. Mum often used to tell me that I would be Miss Australia one day, until her best mate Lois took her aside and warned her that she should stop telling me such lies as clearly I was not Miss Australia material.

But back to the nativity play . . . I didn't even get the roll of a lesser angel. Instead, I was the donkey. As I was steered across the stage alongside Mary and Joseph, my head completely covered by my costume, I didn't have a very good view of the angels. But I heard the cheers and gasps of admiration for Natalie Brown as she led the chorus in a squeaky rendition of 'Silent Night'.

Bitch.

✶

If I wasn't a star of the kindergarten stage, at least I nailed the lot of them when it came to academia. According to my progress report, by April of that first year I was able to recognise the colours red, yellow, blue and green, *and* I had mastered the use of scissors. There was, however, no tick in that box in the social adjustment section, indicating a pupil who 'sulks, cries easily, anxious, tantrums or shy'.

At the end of the year, I received 100 per cent in reading and 100 per cent in mathematics. Under the section *Interested in books and the written word*, Miss Babos had written: *Kayte shows a great deal of interest in books—her enthusiasm in reading and writing is to be commended.*

I positively glowed when Mum read out this comment to me, despite the fact that—my aforementioned interest notwith-standing—I had absolutely no idea what it meant. Enthusiasm? Commended?

So, all in all, kindergarten was a huge year for me. And, despite the hiccup of the nativity play, a successful one. Miss Babos's final report certainly seemed to imply a bright future:

Kayte's achievements in all subject areas are of an excellent standard! Her results in Reading and Mathematics reflect the

PRIMARY SCHOOL CONFIDENTIAL

concentrated effort she makes and the keen interest she shows
in all that she undertakes.

Who was to know that I had already reached my academic
peak?

It was to be all downhill from there.

—2—

SMURFS, SWATCHES AND STRAWBERRY SHORTCAKE

Growing up, there were certain things that you had to possess or risk being cast into social purgatory. These things were the status symbols of the playground. If you were lucky, you had parents who understood the importance of fads and made sure you were furnished with the correct equipment in a timely fashion, meaning you would always be considered cool.

But if, like me, you were one of three kids being brought up by a single working mum who had no time to concern herself with collecting Smurf statuettes from the BP, you would quite often find yourself on the fringes of society, hoping desperately that one of your friends would condescend to let you wear their calculator watch for the second half of lunch.

Oh, don't pity me—I had something that nobody else did. I had a pony. I was a lucky, spoilt girl with a horse. This was thanks to my Poppa, who was famous for breeding slow thoroughbreds. Of course, this meant jack shit in the playground, but I was reminded of the fact each time I requested some new bauble that was all the rage in the playground that week.

The earliest triumph of my superior nagging skills that I can recall was when Mum caved in and wallpapered one wall of my bedroom with Holly Hobbie wallpaper. I was rapt, loving myself sick and inviting all the kids from the neighbourhood to come and bask in the glory that was Holly. (Now, a million years later, it occurs to me that Holly Hobbie was really a very insipid character; she didn't seem to do much other than say naff things and pat her cat while wearing rags. Who knows? Perhaps she was the original crazy cat lady.)

However, at the exact same moment that I had my wall decorated with Holly Hobbie wallpaper, it became socially unacceptable to have even a sniff of anything Holly Hobbie in your possession. It was a good lesson for a six-year-old to learn: you should follow your heart, not follow the pack, and if you loved Holly Hobbie then . . .

Oh, bullshit to that. The pack had moved on and it was all about Strawberry Shortcake. Like Holly Hobbie before her, Strawberry Shortcake stemmed from a character who first made her appearance via greeting cards. And, like Holly, Strawberry Shortcake also had a cat, appropriately named Custard.

In 1980 the doll was launched to much hysteria because she came with the scent of strawberry shortcake. Little girls the world over pestered their parents to buy them this new doll, and then spent hours and hours sniffing them. The company clearly realised they were onto a winner, and soon Strawberry Shortcake was joined by a gaggle of friends, all named after desserts: there was Raspberry Tart, Apple Dumpling and Huckleberry Pie, just to name a few.

My friend Elizabeth was given each new doll by her doting parents as soon as they were released. So, after school, I would come home, get changed out of my uniform and tell my mum: 'I'm just going over to Elizabeth's to smell her dolls, okay?'

And off I would go, cutting through the empty paddock, past the scary man's house, down another suburban street, until I reached her place. Her mum would let me in, make me a Milo and off I would go with Elizabeth, into her room to sniff her doll collection. Lemon Meringue Pie was easily my favourite, and Elizabeth was generous with her fumes, letting me take long, long sniffs of that sickly, synthetic smell.

Soon it was my birthday and I was promised that I would be on the receiving end of a Strawberry Shortcake doll, or at least one of her friends. Naturally, I started bragging about it at school. But to my unspeakable horror, on the day of my birthday I was presented with the most reviled character of the dessert-doll world: the evil and strange Purple Pieman. My stock, which had risen on the promise of entree into the exclusive Shortcake world, abruptly plunged. The Purple Pieman and I were left swinging at the bottom of the social spectrum.

Hey, but at least I had a horse!

That birthday I also received a much-longed-for Western Suburbs Magpies jersey. It went well with my Holly Hobbie wallpaper. I was quite a fucked-up kid, now that I think about it.

But then one day my dad, fresh from an overseas trip, came for a visit and presented me with something new . . . something different . . . something that would blow the other kids' minds. It was a watch, but not just any old watch. It was a Swatch watch. Now, Swatch is said to be a contraction of 'second watch'—but not for me! It was my first-ever watch. It was red, plastic and I was finally an early adapter of a new fad!

I would wear it to school and allow people to admire it. Sometimes, if I was feeling particularly generous, I would let one of the popular kids wear it for the day. But as fads and trends tend to spread like syphilis, it wasn't long until my red watch lost its gloss. Soon, everyone had one.

So, it was back to square one.

Enter . . . Ramona Alvarez.

The Cabbage Patch Kid, a much-hyped and memorable object of desire, came onto the market in 1983 and resulted in parents the world over exhibiting undesirable behaviours in toy stores as they fought to get their hands on one of the precious dolls. By this stage, Mum had met husband number two, a kind and generous fellow who took on Mum, her three kids, two horses, a cat and a geriatric labrador called Sam. They, too, returned from an overseas holiday and presented me and my newly acquired younger step sister with a Cabbage Patch Kid each.

You never really owned a Cabbage Patch Kid; you adopted one. According to the inventor, one Xavier Roberts, each doll was unique and came with an adoption certificate stating that particular doll's name. My doll's name was Ramona Alvarez.

I found it hard to bond with Ramona for a few reasons. One was the ridiculously strange name. Another was that she had red hair. A third reason was that my brother took to using her as a weapon for whacking me and, man, that plastic head was large and hard. Like concrete.

Fucking Ramona Alvarez. Everyone else had blue-eyed, blonde-haired Cabbage Patch Kids with names like Stephanie Joy or Belinda Grace, but not me. Red hair, green eyes and freckles, and a middle name that took me at least a year to learn how to pronounce.

But I had a horse.

Anyway, it was around this time a little-known company called Nintendo introduced something called Game and Watch. Cabbage Patch who?

Game and Watch lived up to its prosaic name. It was a game and a watch. They started popping up in the playground and I can still remember the bright orange of the Donkey Kong game. Through the mists of time (or, rather, from the depths of my booze-soaked brain), I dimly recall that the object of the game was to assist the hero get to the top of the construction site, all the while avoiding the barrels that are being chucked at you by an increasingly angry monkey.

I played Donkey Kong so much that I dreamt about it. Jump. Jump. SPACE SPACE SPACE, up the ladder. Space. Jump. The sequence was the same with every new game. It was the height of technological sophistication at the time.

One craze that was very inclusive—being both cheap and locally available—was the Scanlens football trading cards. You bought them at Gazza's Northo Takeaway (which I believe has since been replaced by Yummy Noodle Bar). They came in packs of three with a stick of gum thrown in for good measure. I was forever searching for the elusive Terry Lamb card to complete my set and have the entire Magpies team represented. It was a cheap hobby, coming in at about twenty cents per pack. And if you had pinched an extra twenty cents from your mum's handbag, you could also avail yourself of a packet of Fags, which were lollies packaged to resemble cigarettes.

I could often be found out the front of Gazza's Northo Takeaway, 'smoking' my fags and trading my cards with other delinquents. And then my older sister would arrive on her bike, telling me that I had to go home and that I was in a ton of trouble because Mrs Brannigan had driven past and seen me standing on the street corner smoking, and she'd rung Mum.

While I was innocent of the alleged crime, it might well have been my penchant for Fags and trading cards that led me down the slippery slope to organised crime . . . And my enabler was an elderly family friend by the name of Judy McGuinness. I liked visiting Judy; she spoilt me rotten and I did not have to compete for her attention with any of my siblings. Judy would let me watch TV whenever I wanted and would give me plates of Iced VoVos and never seemed to get irritated when I followed her around asking question after question, all of which she answered patiently.

Judy used to take me to the local shops with her when she ran errands. We would pick up some groceries, select a cupcake from the bakery and we always visited the chemist to fill prescriptions for Judy's ailing husband, John.

And it was in the chemist that I first stole a hairclip with a ladybird on it.

Later that week, I sold the ladybird hairclip to a girl at school for five cents.

And so began my descent into the world of organised crime. I quickly developed a taste for the good life, and I wanted more. Over the next few months, I continued to visit with Judy, we would go on her errands and I would stuff my pockets with hairclips at the chemist.

One afternoon while Mum was putting away the washing, she came across my latest collection of hair accessories, which were due to hit the market over the next few days. She asked me where I got them from. So I told her that Judy McGuinness had bought them for me.

I was horrified when I saw Mum heading to the telephone and almost died when I heard her say: 'Hi, Judy. I just wanted to thank you . . .'

I ran away. THE JIG WAS UP!

I cautiously entered the kitchen again a few minutes later and heard Mum giving Judy a gentle but firm lecture on how she should not be spending so much money on hair clips for me.

The next time I visited Judy McGuinness, I confessed everything. How could I not? The guilt was overwhelming. She just gave me a hug and told me that we all do stupid things. It made me love her even more. In the meantime, I sold the last of my stock to a cashed-up and willing market and spent the lot on Galaga and Icees, which were the latest fad . . .

THE BENEFITS OF A STATION WAGON

I asked a friend of mine, fellow blogger Kirsten Smith, if she had a stand-out memory from her primary school days. And she did.

I absolutely loved school as a kid, which was just as well because I went to six of them: four primary schools and two high schools. I wish there was an exciting story to tell about the reason behind the rather large number of school enrolment forms my parents, Pam and Errol Woolcott, have completed over the years but, unfortunately, there's not.

I'd love to be able to tell you that at 2 pm on a cold winter's day in 1984, Pam and Errol were summoned to the principal's office to discuss my behaviour where the imaginary conversation went a little something like this:

'Mr and Mrs Woolcott, please have a seat. Let me just move this ashtray out of the way and I'll be able to find your daughter's file.' Principal picks up brown glass ashtray and places it next to typewriter. Looks down at desk. 'Ah, yes. Here it is,' he says, picking up a thick manila folder and wiping cigarette ash from the front of it.

'I keep telling my secretary to get me one of those new ashtrays on a stand that traps the ash inside. Have you seen them? Such a clever contraption. The mind boggles at what they will invent next!'

Sits down and opens file. 'Now, as you're aware, our resident Anglican nun, Sister Bridget, teaches the children Religious Education once a week.'

'Oh, yes,' Pam might answer. 'Lovely lady. Has the perfect skin tone for someone who has to wear black all day long!'

Principal raises eyebrows, looks up over glasses and clears throat. 'Mrs Woolcott, this is not the time or the place to be discussing a nun's skin tone. I have called you and Mr Woolcott here today because your daughter, Kirsten, has done something very serious that will more than likely see her expelled from this school.'

'That doesn't surprise me. What did she do this time?' Errol might reply. 'Please tell me she didn't sneak her pet rabbit into her backpack again. Pam, I thought you were checking her bag in the mornings?'

Cue a hefty glare thrown at Errol from Pam and a loud sigh from the principal, followed by the words, 'No, she did not bring the rabbit to school again. She did however call Sister Bridget, Sister Birdshit, not once but TWICE during Religious Education this morning.'

'OH MY GOD. Where the bloody hell would she have gotten language like that from?! Jesus Christ. I'll kill her when I get my hands on her. Sister Birdshit. I'll give her bloody birdshit. She's a nun forchristsakes. You can't talk like that to a nun!'

'Fairly sure you can't talk like that in a principal's office either, Pam,' Errol might say as he stands up and eyeballs Pam to do the same. 'Thank you, Mr Walker, for your time. We will collect Kirsten and her belongings on our way out.'

Mr Walker stands up from behind his desk, 'Thank you, Mr Woolcott. I would appreciate that. Oh, there's just one last thing before you go.'

'Yes?' Pam might ask as she smooths out the wrinkles on her high-waisted polyester slacks.

'My wife was admiring your hair the other day when our boys were playing soccer and she asked me to enquire, if I may, where you get it permed?'

But, no, there were never any phone calls from the school to my parents or suspensions or expulsions, although I did have a pet rabbit and was, on occasion, taught by a nun whose name was Sister Bridget. She was known in the playground as Sister Birdshit, although I can neither confirm nor deny that the person responsible for coming up with that nickname was in fact a ten-year-old me.

The real, slightly boring reason for attending six schools in twelve years of education was because my parents liked to move a lot. That's it. Which isn't quite as exciting as an imaginary conversation in the principal's office about swearing at a nun, but it does make for several actual interesting stories, including the time our class went on an excursion.

The primary school I was a student at the longest was a lovely little inner city one in Christchurch, New Zealand. It had a beautiful old stone building that housed the classrooms, a timber church next door and approximately no grass to play on.

Each day, Mum used to drive my brother Blair and me to and from school in her pale-blue mini, which had a tendency to not start in the mornings ('Get in kids and cross your fingers she starts today!'), while Dad drove the school excursion jackpot—a station wagon, which was a recent addition to our household.

In Year 4, or Standard Two as it was known in New Zealand in 1981, there was much excitement among our class of twenty-seven students when our teacher Mrs Hill announced we would be going on our very first excursion to inspect an aeroplane hangar of all things. Parent volunteers were required to assist getting us all to and from the venue, otherwise we wouldn't be able to go, and could you please put your hand up if any of your parents drive a station wagon?

Now up until this point, I had spent a vast amount of the lesson daydreaming about bean bags. You see my friend Diane, who lived up the road from me, had just had a bean bag made for her bedroom. It was quite an odd shape but it was made from the most luxurious purple fabric I'd ever felt.

'It's corduroy,' Diane informed me, as I gently ran my hands across the softly woven fabric. 'Most people use it to make overalls but Mum said it would make a terrific bean bag. It's filled with tiny little balls of foam. You can sit on it if you like.'

21

I stopped touching the fabric and stared at the purple corduroy-covered bean bag sitting on the thick brown shag-pile carpet in the corner of Diane's bedroom. 'Diane, you are so lucky. This is the coolest thing I've ever seen. It would be so good to sit in one of these after rollerskating every Saturday!'

I tried to sit down gracefully on the bean bag—but graceful isn't really a word that springs to mind when describing my athletic abilities—so instead I slipped on the one-inch thick shag-pile carpet, fell backwards onto the bean bag and accidentally let out a fart at the exact moment my butt hit the soft foam-filled fabric.

This was followed by a few seconds of awkward silence before Diane yelled, 'Did you just fart on my bean bag?' Her face all twisted into an unusual look of horror and disgust.

I started laughing, which didn't exactly help the situation, while Diane shouted, 'Mum! Kirsten just farted on my bean bag!'

Diane's Mum entered the room and calmly assessed the situation. She took one look at a red-faced Diane, then one look at me laughing hysterically on the bean bag, and very politely suggested that it might be best for all concerned if I made my way back home.

Probably a fair call. I mean it was corduroy and I did just fart on it. I thanked Diane's Mum for having me, apologised to Diane, put my pink jelly shoes on and walked home.

On my way home I decided that I was really lucky Diane didn't go to my school because, if she did, there was a fairly high chance I would be known as the girl who farted on a bean bag for the rest of my life. I also decided that I really, really wanted a bean bag of my own.

The only problem was that Mum didn't have a sewing machine and I'd already put in a request for a Cabbage Patch Kid, a game of Guess Who? and a View-Master for Christmas, so I thought adding a corduroy bean bag to the list might've been pushing things a bit.

However—back to the classroom—upon hearing Mrs Hill say the words 'excursion' and 'station wagon' snapped me right out of my bean bag daydream and my hand went up quicker than a contestant on *The Price Is Right*!

'Mrs Hill! Mrs Hill! My dad has a station wagon!' I shouted excitedly, while frantically waving my hand around.

'It's a red one. He just got it. Although it's not really his. I think his boss is lending it to him? I'm not sure. Dad told us about it while we were eating tea last night but I wasn't really listening because Mum had cooked schnitzel and it's my favourite and she hardly ever makes it and—'

'Thank you, Kirsten—' Mrs Hill interrupted (that used to happen to me a lot during primary school)—'for yet another very in-depth answer to a fairly simple question. I think your father might have what is known as a company car,' continued Mrs Hill, while no doubt wondering how quickly a cigarette lighter works in a new station wagon and if those new beige vinyl seats everyone keeps talking about really are as slippery to sit on as they say they are. 'I'll give your dad a call at lunch time and see if he is allowed to use it for a school excursion.'

Turns out Dad was allowed to use the work station wagon for school excursions and, while we were all in the playground inhaling peanut butter sandwiches and playing Red Rover on the concrete, Mrs Hill was working hard in the staffroom, calling other parents to ask if they too had a station wagon and would they like to join us on an excursion?

By the time we all filed back into our classroom at the end of lunch, Mrs Hill had successfully managed to rope two other parents into using their station wagons, so the excursion was happening!

'Right,' said Mrs Hill as she whipped out a piece of chalk from her hair. 'It's time for a quick maths lesson. Eyes on the board!'

We all stared straight ahead as Mrs Hill proceeded to write the following sum in longhand on the large blackboard on the wall:

If there are twenty-seven students in a class who are going on an excursion and there are three station wagons to take them to and from the venue, how many children will fit in each car?

I was never any good at maths, so I watched on as hands shot up around me and someone yelled out, 'Nine! There will be nine of us in each car!'

'That's right, Mark,' said Mrs Hill. 'Well done. There will be nine of you in each car. One in the front seat, three in the back seat and five in the boot.'

'Where will you be, Mrs Hill?' asked Kelly.

'Oh, I will be driving in my own car behind you all, keeping an eye on things and making sure everyone is safe. Now if you could pass these notes around and make sure your parents read them, please. It explains everything they need to know about the excursion. Oh, and if you're short, you're in luck. You'll be riding in the boot of the station wagons to and from the excursion because it will be easier for you sit on your bottom and cross your legs in such a cramped space!'

If you don't count the day I received a free Wombles poster with my book club order, this was the most exciting day of my primary school life. Not only was my dad coming with me on my very first excursion but, thanks to being one of the shortest members of the class, I was going to ride in the boot of a station wagon with four of my vertically challenged friends! If only I had a corduroy bean bag to sit on to make the ride more comfortable . . .

Visit Kirsten at her blog @ kirstenandco.com.

THE PRIDE OF ERIN

Of all the things I learned in primary school, the one thing I remember most clearly to this day is how to dance the Pride of Erin. I cannot recall the capital of Peru, and I still can't work out the symbols for 'less than' and 'more than', but if you need to know the steps to the Pride of Erin—or even the Heel and Toe Polka, for that matter—I'm your gal.

Dancing lessons at school. Do you know that they were actually part of the curriculum back then? Depending on your vintage, you may have learnt anything from the Bullockies Ball to the Jubilee Jig, the Prince of Wales Schottische to the Waterfall Waltz.

Our dancing lesson, if memory serves me correct (and it does seem to favour days of yore), was on a Thursday afternoon. We all filed into the hall, with the boys lined up on one side and the girls on the other. It was like a Mexican stand-off.

The teacher would then ask the boys to choose a partner. (CAN YOU FUCKING BELIEVE THAT? DO YOU KNOW WHAT THAT DOES TO A GIRL WITH COKE-BOTTLE GLASSES

AND TEETH THAT PROTRUDE FROM HER MOUTH AT A NINETY-DEGREE ANGLE?) All the boys would rush to the pretty girls and grab them by the hand. And I stood there, like a lonely sausage in the meat display window of a butcher's shop at the end of the day.

So I ended up dancing with the strange girl who wouldn't talk to anyone, but just picked at her scabs and ate them.

Thankfully, the Pride of Erin was a progressive dance, and I got to have actual physical contact with the male species. Which was all very well and good until you ended up dancing with the cool, cute boy who refused to touch you because someone spread a rumour that you had warts.

You then moved on to Stanley, whom you refused to touch because back in kindergarten he shat his pants and sat in it all day and was referred to as Stinky Stanley ever since. Oh, the politics of progressive dance!

Then, after all the formal dancing, the teachers let you go apeshit by blaring 'Nutbush City Limits', which was when your creativity could finally be unleashed—but not really, as you had to do the correct moves or were made to go and sit on the stage, alone, like a renegade disco diva who had lost her way.

But disco was an exotic byway; the main game was the good old Aussie bush dance, and in the 1980s our bible was *The Bushwhackers Band Dance Book*. It was from this much-loved and well-thumbed resource that Mr Ellis or Mr Lewis taught us how to dance the Waves of Bondi. Looking back on that experience, it must have been as fun for them as it is to try to bathe a cat. Apparently, when the dance is done correctly, it resembles waves crashing onto Bondi Beach.

Apparently.

It was somewhat creepy to watch your teacher dance with Mrs Hunt on the stage, pleading with you to watch on and learn each little step. The truth of the fact was that we thought these dances were daggy, and we would much rather learn the steps to 'Thriller'.

My fondness for the art of dance saw me and my two best friends, Penny and Audra, start our own little dance trio. We were awfully exclusive and practised a lot each afternoon after school.

There were two stand-out numbers that we concentrated on. The first was a mysterious and exotic song and dance performed to the tune of 'Magic', sung by Olivia Newton-John in the wonderful movie *Xanadu*.

Penny's mum, Mrs Riley, was very encouraging, and she proved to be quite nifty with a sewing machine. For this dance, we wore pink and purple dresses that had handkerchief hems— the glamour! They looked very floaty and dramatic when we held the bottoms of our dresses and swirled suggestively around the stage.

We debuted our act at the school's quarterly talent quest, and came a respectable second place behind the boy who did the Frank Carpenter impersonation. (However, the principal did tell us that our performance was a little too adult.) Buoyed by our success, we immediately began work on a new number in preparation for the following term's quest.

'Walking on Sunshine' by Katrina and the Waves had just been released. It was upbeat, catchy and definitely less creepy than 'Magic'. Mrs Riley made us costumes again, and they too were much less controversial. We wore sunny yellow halterneck dresses with sensible knee-length hems.

We were positively giddy with excitement at the prospect of winning the school talent quest and, if the reaction of the enraptured crowd was anything to go by, our victory was assured.

But while we'd been feverishly rehearsing our dance number, a rival had been equally busy at the piano. Susie Jarski took to the stage and stole the limelight, playing Beethoven's 'Für Elise' without a single mistake.

And so, to the victor went the spoils. Susie won a $2 voucher to the canteen. (It was probably for the best, as it would have been hard to split that two bucks between three people. Although, I suppose we could have bought 200 carob buds and divvied them up that way . . .)

But the thing was, for all the effort we put into our dance trio—the time, the rehearsals, the choreography, the costume fittings, the drama, the disagreements about who got to be in the middle—it was never about the prize. We just wanted to be known throughout the school as talented.

Through all my primary school years—and I am ready to admit this now—I never won a thing. Oh, sure, I got a merit award here and there, but that doesn't really count. (Insider secret: everyone in the class has to get one over the course of the year; it is an unwritten rule.)

But if I never won, there was a time when I came second—and it was fucking marvellous.

I was in Year 1, and Easter was approaching—and with it the annual hat parade. Most of my schoolmates had stay-at-home mums who probably relished the chance to pit their creative skills against each other. But my mother was time-poor. She was working her ring off trying to build her new business, Christine Murphy's Indoor Plant Hire. Basically she was, and still is, excellent with plants, and she established the first indoor plant-hire business in Australia. For a couple of dollars a week, she would supply and tend to plants in businesses and restaurants.

I knew Mum didn't have the time to create a fancy hat for the parade but, undeterred, I entered the 'I Made It Myself' category, designed for those children who would be responsible for making their own bonnets.

Looking around our house, it was fairly evident that we were not a crafty family. We had no magical cupboard full of pipe cleaners, special tape and glue. We had a few textas and that was about it. So I had to be quite experimental. I waited patiently until the pink ice-cream was finally eaten from the Neopolitan ice-cream selection, and then I swiped the plastic container. I covered it in tin foil, then pasted on a few hand-drawn pictures of rabbits.

Stick a fork in me . . . I was DONE.

The big day arrived and I proudly wore my hat to school. I was surprised to find that many of the other kids weren't wearing hats. When I asked why, they explained that their mothers were bringing them in at recess because they were too intricate and fragile to be used as everyday wear.

After recess the parade began, and to give credit where it is due, the mothers at North Richmond Public School that year had completely outdone themselves. Parading around the grass were wonderful examples of just what you can do with a glue gun.

Mine was the last category to be called on. Me and another boy walked around for a little bit, then he was given a blue ribbon and I was given a red one.

Sweet rapturous joy flooded through me. I was a winner! And I did it myself!

It totally made up for the fact that, as it turned out later, I couldn't dance for shit.

—4—

PRETTY IN FLUORO PINK

Like most girls of my age, my first interest in fashion and appearance can be traced back to one person: Madonna.

When she burst onto the world stage in the early 1980s, she redefined fashion for me. Want to wear some bike pants under a miniskirt with a ripped t-shirt over another ripped t-shirt under a mesh singlet? Be my guest. Better still, pile on every single bracelet and bangle in your house and you were really good to go. Even if it was just a trip to Coles with your mum to do the grocery shopping, you were going to rock those aisles.

There was just one problem: my parents had no intention of allowing their pre-teen daughter to parade around town dressed like some sort of hooker. And so I was an oppressed child stuck in sensible shorts and a t-shirt with a picture of a pony on it.

Meanwhile, my sister, who was three years older and worked after school at Marie's Record Magic, earned her own money and was able to spend it as she pleased. She bought super-cool things like blue eyeliner, blue eyeshadow, frosted pink lipstick and mesh singlets. She was a bitch about sharing, too. Not to worry. As soon as she left the house to do whatever horrendous teenage girls do (i.e. smoke cigarettes in the park with the other juvenile delinquents), I would make a beeline straight for her room.

Armed with the latest issue of *Smash Hits* for reference, I would use all of my sister's makeup to emulate either Madonna or Cyndi Lauper, another style icon of mine. And I didn't bother with subtlety, no way. I stacked it on. I'd start with two big swipes of hot pink blush that ran from the corners of my mouth, up and over my cheekbones to end at my earlobes. My eyes were lined with electric-blue pencil while the lids were liberally dusted with a matching powder and my eyelashes caked in mascara in the same shade. To counterbalance the look, I painted my lips with Revlon's Pink in the Afternoon, a shimmery pale pink that I believe is still available today.

Next it was time for hair and wardrobe. I'd tip my head upside down and tease my hair until it resembled a halo around my head. Clipped to my ears were a pair of huge white hoops. My sister had an impressive wardrobe, and I would put on basically everything she owned, for layering was de rigueur. Finally, with my feet swimming around in her Doc Martens, the concert would commence.

I used my pink tape deck to record my favourite songs from the American Top 40. I would grab my hairbrush, hit play, and imagine myself standing on a stage, singing and dancing in front of thousands of screaming fans.

Because I was a professional, there was light and shade to my performance. I might start out with Irene Cara's 'Flashdance . . . What a Feeling', which was always a crowd pleaser. Then I'd slow things with a heart-felt rendition of 'Total Eclipse of the Heart'. I'd then change the tempo with a series of upbeat numbers like 'Beat It', 'Holiday' and 'Girls Just Want to Have Fun' until, finally, I was discovered. Not by a recording agent keen to listen to my demo, but by my sister. And she was not in the mood for fun.

Down the stairs I'd race, her hot on my heels. If I was lucky, I'd make it to wherever my mother was and thus be saved. If I was unlucky, I'd cop a generous beating and a spray of language so foul it would have made a bikie blush.

By the time I hit Year 6, my interest in couture was stronger than ever. So Mum eventually relented to my pleas and took me on a shopping trip to Grace Bros at Penrith Plaza. Until then, all my clothes shopping had been done in the children's wear department, but not anymore. Mum took me to the Miss Shop and I was in heaven.

The racks were crammed with fluorescent clothing and I wanted to play a big part in this trend. I wanted to *own* this trend. I could not get enough of the fluorescent stuff so we pulled an outfit together that would let the general public know that I fully endorsed this fashion moment.

Fluoro pink jeans, fluoro green top, two studded belts (orange and yellow) that were tied together and went around my hips twice. And the pièce de résistance? Two pairs of fluoro socks, worn in such a way that, when folded down, both colours were displayed!

Magic happened in the change room that day, my friends. Magic.

We took our items to the counter to pay for them. Mum pulled out her credit card. Then, just as she was about to hand it over, she paused.

'What is it, Mum?' I asked anxiously.

'I think you need this . . .' she replied. And then she handed me—get this—MY VERY FIRST LIPSTICK OF MY OWN!

It was gorgeous. A very shiny tube in the shape of a bullet. Inside was the thickest, brightest pink shade that was ever made. I swear it was almost radioactive. I almost fainted with glee. I hugged Mum tight and told her that I was the happiest girl in the whole world. But deep down I knew there was one thing that would make me even happier.

If I could make my sister envious, my life would be complete.

When I got home, I got dressed in my new clothes. I teased my fringe until it stood straight up on end. I ever so carefully applied my hot-pink lippie. I was ready.

I knocked on my sister's door and entered her room. She was lying on her bed reading a *Dolly* magazine. She glanced up from the pages and gave me the once-over before declaring that I looked like a retard* and going back to her reading.

I was not crushed, however, as she was going through a goth phase, which meant she spent her time listening to The Cure, dying her hair black (much to the chagrin of the oldies), and wearing black on black on black. She was also basically non-verbal to everyone in the house. Mum kept saying something about hormones and we all gradually learnt not to poke the beast.

---

* A super-offensive term, but one that was used frequently during my youth.

There was one other day, one other glorious day that I will never forget, which cemented my passage into being a fashion victim forever. Mum and I were shopping at Penrith Plaza when I came across something so fantastic, I was rendered speechless.

A pair of white lace ankle boots.

It was like there was a light beaming down on them from the ceiling of Grace Bros, and they were calling to me. I picked them up and inspected them from every angle. They were perfect. Like something Madonna would try to steal from me if I were ever to go to one of her live shows and she somehow caught a glimpse of my feet.

It was apparently a perfect storm of my mum's generous mood and my lack of speech that saw me skipping through the front door of our house later that afternoon wearing the most marvellous boots the world had ever seen. Even my sisters were completely jealous.

I finally owned something enviable.

I told everyone at school about my boots, and the next week, Lynette Bitch Face and her mother went off to Penrith Plaza and bought the very same ones. But we were not allowed to be mean to Lynette because her brother was in jail, so I had to just cop that one on the chin.

Pretty soon nearly every girl in my class had the Madonna Lace Boots and we all wore them to the school social, giving pitying looks to those girls who were wearing Apple Pies.

My mum sometimes fancied herself as a fashion designer, so when the puffball skirt craze hit and I showed her a photo of Madonna wearing one in *Smash Hits*, and asked if we could get one from Sportsgirl, she waved the magazine away and told me that she could whip one up for me.

I wanted a black one, but she objected, telling me I was too young to wear black. Instead she made me a puffball skirt out of a pale blue grosgrain material. The skirt was not puffy. It was limp. Saggy might be a good word to describe it. A saggy, limp skirt. I wasn't a fan. But this didn't mean I was against homemade clothes per se. It was around this time that a film came out featuring homemade clothes that seemed to me the epitome of high fashion: *Pretty in Pink*. This film would also mark the zenith of my obsession with the combined oeuvre of filmmaker John Hughes and actor Molly Ringwald.

In each film Molly played a girl who was 'different' but who nevertheless ended up with the cute guy. Molly was Sam Baker in *Sixteen Candles* and, while she was pissed off that everyone forgot her birthday, she did get to pash foxy Jake Ryan in the end.

She was Claire Standish in *The Breakfast Club*, which was about a group of kids who were on detention. Her character was snooty and standoffish. A lot of this film went way over my head at the time, but I always appreciated a makeover scene.

But my absolute favourite film was *Pretty in Pink*, in which Molly played Andie Walsh, a motherless waif from the wrong side of the tracks who made all her own clothes and they were cool and quirky. Andie became the target of the school jock when she dared to reject his advances; she had her eyes on another prize, said jock's best mate, a preppy lad by the name of Blane McDonnagh, played by Andrew McCarthy. Blane was not handsome in a traditional sense, and neither was Andie.

Despite all the obstacles standing in their way, love blossomed between them.

My first experience of loin-stirrage occurred when Blane asked Andie to the prom and they went for the big tongue-slurping kiss. Looking back on that scene now, you can really see how awkward and unsexy it was, but at the time it was like someone had released a dozen drunk butterflies directly into my guts. I wanted to be kissed like that.

I also wanted to unpick a couple of dresses and put them back together. But I was not allowed to use Mum's Singer . . . because I didn't know how to sew.

If *Pretty in Pink* had any legacy to leave, it was the sexual awakening of millions of girls. I was not alone in my quest to be kissed like that but, unlike some of the other girls, it would be years before someone stuck their tongue down my throat.

So I had to make do with practising on my pillow.

DON'T YOU DARE SIT THERE JUDGING ME! I bet you did it too. Or perhaps you might have pashed wall posters as well. Wall posters of Boy George even.

Don't worry. I won't tell anyone.

Which is such bullshit. After one particular slumber party, during which I displayed my superior kissing techniques, complete with correct hand placement, word got around the school that I had pashed my pillow—even though all the girls present had taken the secret oath of the sisterhood never to tell.

Kids can be so cruel. I just wanted to have some intimate time with my pillow, and share my knowledge with the other girls, and all of a sudden I was a laughing-stock. I deeply regretted being so generous with my knowledge. I'm sure that's the reason no boys wanted to kiss me in primary school. Which was quite frustrating at the time, because I was becoming more aware of boys—and more aware of myself and what others thought of me. I was about to enter the cruel world of primary school politics . . .

5

SOCIAL DEATH

For many readers, to mention 1984 is to evoke George Orwell's eerily prescient dystopian novel. For music lovers it might evoke the soundtrack album by the Eurythmics. But, for me, 1984 will always be remembered as the year *Countdown* first screened Madonna's hit song 'Holiday'. That Sunday night changed my life forever. I had never seen someone so cool, so gorgeous and so funky. I shoved Ramona Alvarez into the back of my wardrobe and fell head over heels in love with the world of pop singers.

It's no coincidence that 1984 was also the year that *Smash Hits* magazine was first published in Australia. I was on board from day one. I would save all the pocket money I earned by picking up dogshit in the backyard and every second Friday I would pop off to the newsagency to get my copy.

I became a collector of compilation cassette tapes and would proudly line up my copies of *1984 Shakin'*, *H'its Huge '84* and *Throbbin' 84*, fully believing that the blatant abuse of the apostrophe thought up by some dipshit in the marketing department of Polygram was actually cool. I would listen to the tapes over and over and over again on my new red Walkman while flicking through the latest issue of *Smash Hits*.

In 1984 I was in Year 5 at school and things were changing for me. I started looking in the mirror a little more, wondering why I didn't look like Madonna. Boys were becoming less of a nuisance and more interesting to me, while my parents were becoming less interesting and starting to give me the legitimate shits.

I was learning, too, that the world was unfair in many respects. I discovered to my horror that millions of Ethiopians were starving to death; thank God that my virtual gods were able to sing a song about it and save the planet.

I found it to be grossly unfair that the teenagers of a small town somewhere in the Midwest of the United States were forbidden to dance, and breathed a huge sigh of relief when Ren, the kid from Chicago, challenged the small town's small minds with some canny quotes from the Bible and the school prom was able to take place after all. (That Ren proceeds to suck face with Ariel, the rebellious daughter of the anti-dancing reverend, was a delightfully ironic twist!)

And I fell in love for the very first time, with a small and quite creepy-looking chap who went by the name of Prince. Because he was funky.

I longed to go to the Entertainment Centre and see Joe Cocker or The Police, but my oldies were not having a bar of it, which is not to say they were averse to culture. They took the family to see Torvill and Dean on ice and any number of Andrew Lloyd Webber musicals.

There is nothing worse for someone on the cusp of becoming a teenager than spending time with her family. Each evening, my family would come together to eat at the dinner table. This was extremely annoying, as all my friends got to eat dinner in front of the television. However, it did set the stage for my older sister—already a fully-fledged teenager—to throw her nightly temper tantrum. You could set your clock by it. Sullen and sulky, she would sit at the table glowering, pushing her specially prepared vegetarian meal around on her plate. Inevitably, someone would say something to her and, however innocuous, she would crack the shits. Heated words would be spat out like bullets from an AK-47, a punishment threatened, and then she would dramatically push her chair back, and run up the stairs and into her room. The scene would end with a very loud slamming of the door. Observing the evolution of a teenager was both fascinating and terrifying, and total respect to my oldies, who rode that wild ride five times.

As I began to develop my own taste in music and fashion (taste that was hardly unique, I have to admit), I was starting to become aware that trends and fads were different when you were at the pointy end of primary school. Image started to play an important role. Wearing your hair the right way. Wearing the right socks. Not being different. Going with the flow. Not questioning the playground powerbrokers. Toeing the line. It is a sad fact that these years can shape the sort of person that you turn out to be, unless you have the confidence to stand on your own two feet.

But I wasn't one of those people! I wanted to belong and was acutely aware of what could happen if you dared question the establishment: social death.

I would see it happen all the time. The worst thing was to be excluded from someone's birthday party. Birthday parties were a huge deal, easily the highlight of the Year 5 social scene. Looking back, there is one in particular that stands out.

Sally Griffin's slumber party.

We had spent the afternoon tearing about, dancing to INXS and Michael Jackson, talking about boys, eating crap and watching *Back to the Future*. When it came time to sleep, well, we were not having a bar of it!

At 11 pm Mrs Griffin appeared at the door of the rumpus room and pleaded with us to be quiet.

At 1 am Mrs Griffin returned, and threatened to shut the party down via several urgent phone calls to our parents.

At 4 am Mr Griffin barged through the door and completely lost his shit.

The thing about Mr Griffin was that he was Scottish and his accent was thicker than pea soup. The more he yelled, the redder his face got. His tirade went something along the lines of: 'Listen up, ye wee shits. Ahm gonnae kick yer behinds intae next week unless ye gang tae sleep. Ah hae tae gie up fur wark in tois hoors, ye wee fuckers. Noo jobby th' buck up.'

And I swear I heard someone urinate in her pants.

Sleep came quickly after that for most, but not me. I snuggled into my sleeping bag, too frightened to move. It was only as the sun came up, and I heard Mr Griffin go off to work, that I could finally exhale.

I remember the next day was very long, and I was very tired and emotional, so much so that Sally Griffin's was the last slumber party I was allowed to go to for a long time.

But back to social death. I experienced it for exactly two days in Year 6 and will never forget the dreadful feeling that comes with being on the outer. You see, my friend and I—subject to peer pressure—had choked on a cigarette with a couple of high school boys. When this news travelled back to the playground, we were instant social pariahs. We were BANISHED from the traditional game of handball that was the measure of social standing.

Our so-called friends decided that if we were to play with them and they should accidentally touch us, they would immediately die from cancer. It was a very upsetting state of affairs, and one that I could not share with my parents for obvious reasons. For two days my friend and I spent recess and lunchtime sitting in the library and reading the rude bits of a Judy Blume book aloud to each other. Then another kid wet her pants (probably the same one who'd wet her pants at Sally Griffin's slumber party the year before), so we got swapped back in. But we had learnt our lesson: don't rock the boat.

6

YOUNG LOVE (OF THE NON-EQUINE KIND)

I grew up surrounded by horses, as Dad was a bigwig in the racing industry and my Poppa was a famed breeder of the world's slowest thoroughbreds. A few times I was the recipient of one of the backward runners, which I used to then take to pony club and ride alongside my peers. While they bounced around on their Shetland ponies, I would be galloping around on a horse that was fresh off the track. I won any event that involved speed. Not because my horse was particularly fast, just because it was eleven times the size of the others.

I recall one summer, a KFC store opened up, causing much excitement because there was a drive-thru. An actual drive-thru! KFC was called by its full name, Kentucky Fried Chicken, back then, because everyone still believed that fried chicken was healthy.

I was in my swimmers, in the pool, when I had a sudden craving for hot chips. I think I would have been about ten. Those hot-chip cravings have been around a long time, and remain a part of my life to this day.

Anyway, I jumped out of the pool, stole a couple of bucks from Mum's wallet and headed down to the paddock, swinging a halter and lead in my hand. I then proceeded to ride my horse, which was about seventeen hands high, through the streets—navigating some very busy intersections—and into the drive-thru, where I ordered some hot chips with extra salt. The slack-jawed teenagers serving could hardly believe their eyes. I took the hot chips down to the river, hoovered them up, then treated Abby the horse to a little swim. I did all this without the benefit of a helmet. Or a saddle. Or any sense whatsoever.

Horses were my first love, closely followed by hot chips. But that was about to all change for me.

The first time a boy ever told me that he loved me I was all of seven years old. We had only known each other for two days. He looked me in the eyes and said confidently, 'I love you, Kelly.'

Which was fine by me, even though my name was, and still is, Kayte. But, hey, he was cute and someone loved me and so I was Kelly for the next twenty-four hours until the end of that pony club camp.

I didn't think about boys for a few years, then all of a sudden they were all I could think about! I flew through a handful of crushes. There was Lance, who looked like a sheep, so thick and curly was his white-blond hair. And then there was Christopher, with whom I was quite smitten until my mum remarried and we moved towns. So he was gone (though, clearly, not forgotten).

By the time I reached Year 5, if you didn't have a boyfriend you were considered a complete loser. I wished not to be a complete loser and by this stage I had, fortunately, lost my Coke-bottle glasses, my hair looked relatively normal and my teeth had decided to straighten themselves out. The only problem was I was quite tall for my age, and all the boys were midgets. But this was a minor impediment. I wouldn't say that I was in the running to win the *Dolly* Covergirl competition, but I was not a complete cretin either.

So I put the word out via my little gang of friends that I was ready to 'go with' someone. (The term 'go with' was the vernacular at the time and the ironic thing was that you ended up going nowhere. It was just a label.) It was like I was putting out a request to tender for the role of my boyfriend. At recess and lunch, interested suitors were put forward.

'Alan said he would go with you,' came the word.

And I would be all like, 'Alan! He has fricking warts!'

Next!

'Peter said he would go with you.'

Sweet Mary, mother of GOD! Peter shat in his pants two years ago. Was this it for me? Was I already scraping the bottom of the barrel at the age of eleven?

'Paul said he would go with you.'

'Ryan or Waters?'

'Paul Ryan in Year 6.'

And that is how I got my first boyfriend.

Now that I had my boyfriend, what was I supposed to do with him?

The answer, my friends, was handball. Using chalk, a huge grid was drawn up on the concrete with allocated spots for King,

Queen, Jack and Dunce. We played mixed doubles, with each square accommodating one happy couple.

I was a very good handball player and Paul proved to be a good match for me in that department. We didn't speak much. Just played handball a lot.

The relationship, perhaps due to its non-verbal nature, failed to thrive. But little did I know just how bad things had got. Shortly after acquiring my first boyfriend, I would find myself on the receiving end of my first dumping.

It all started on a school excursion. As usual, everyone raced to the back of the bus, trampling smaller ones who got in their way. I was not that concerned about sitting at the back of the bus, so took my seat about halfway down the aisle. Word travelled down to me that Paul had saved me a seat at the back of the bus.

He wanted me to sit next to him? Who was he fucking kidding? No WAY!

This act of independence proved to be my undoing. The next day, in the playground at recess, one of Paul's mates told my friend Penny that Paul wanted to break up with me. Penny delivered the bad news to me, and I fled to the girls' toilets for the rest of eternity.

Eternity lasted until the end-of-recess bell, which rang out precisely seven minutes later. I had a choice to make: I could remain sobbing in the bathroom, a victim of public humiliation, or I could straighten myself out, splash some water on my face and bravely take my place in the class line. Which is what I did.

I joined the Year 5 line while Paul stood nearby in the Year 6 line. I looked across and down at him, and when I caught his eye, I mouthed slowly and deliberately: 'I hate you.'

And with those three little words, I was over him. Little fucker. I spent the rest of the year trying to spread rumours that Paul

Ryan had stinky breath and wet his pants, and anything else I could think of that would shame him.

★

As the school year went by, I became friends with boys. It was nice. It gave me the confidence to be myself in front of them—and let's face it, I was more of a tomboy than a girly girl up until that point. There was a little group of us, boys and girls, who hung out a fair bit. And then hormones came and reared their ugly head and eventually everyone had paired up with someone to 'go with'.

My new boyfriend was a deadset spunk and a nice boy to boot. My mum knew his mum, who was one of the local swimming instructors. He proved to be a very good handball player. And I actually *did* want to sit next to him at the back of the bus, where we would hold hands. He had no warts. Nice clean hands.

We became the king and queen of handholding. Everywhere we went, we'd be swinging digits. Up the back of the hall in assembly, we would sit side by side. He would put out his hand for me to hold, and so I did.

Then we went to see *Ghostbusters* at the Richmond Regent and it was here that things heated up a bit. An actual arm went out and snaked around my shoulders. Of course I could not concentrate on the movie. A cute boy had his arm around me! It took all my concentration not to wet my pants there in the seat. During the interval, when he went to get me a treat from the the kiosk, I shared this new development with my friends, who were seated on my other side. I was so happy!

Our relationship flourished. Our friends were constantly splitting up and swapping partners in dramatic fashion, but not us! We were like the Paul Newman and Joanne Woodward of the playground. He would shower me with gifts. Like, one time, he presented me with a plastic bag which contained a car seat for my Cabbage Patch Kid, Ramona Alvarez. He gave me a bracelet with my name engraved on the outside and his name engraved on the inside, which may have just made my heart stop.

And then, of course, came my first-ever kiss! I was such a fan of the experience that I went on to do quite a bit of kissing as a teenager. But that first kiss . . . you never forget it. Even if it happened when you were twelve. Even if it was in front of all your friends, with them egging you on.

We were at a party, which was a slumber party for both boys and girls. I KNOW! But the fun police (my parents) refused to let me attend the actual sleepover part, so I just went along for the movie section of the festivities. We did our traditional handholding, and the now customary arm around the shoulder. We were getting a *lot* of peer pressure to pucker up and so, after a lot of nagging, we eventually did, giving each other a small peck on the lips.

The crowd EXPLODED!

Looking back on it now, it was quite perverted, but I felt that we were ready to take our relationship to the next level, so along with handholding and arms around the shoulders, we added quick kisses to our repertoire of PDAs.

Then, as tended to happen in those days, the old bush tele-graph kicked into gear and word got back to my parents, who promptly enrolled me in a boarding school for my high school years. I presume they were thinking that this might save me from myself. I cannot say for sure that their decision was made on the basis of a few quick, dry pecks on the lips, but I suspect said kisses didn't help my cause.

YOUNG LOVE (OF THE NON-EQUINE KIND)

As the year drew to an end, Mum took me to the local children's wear shop, which was extraordinarily fashion forward for the time. There I chose the most perfect outfit for the Year 6 farewell. It was a pale pink dress that was teamed with a short-sleeved floral jacket. On my feet I wore a pair of white leather shoes. I had been taken to Toppings, the local hairdressers, where I was given a blow wave of brilliance. Never before had I ever been able to tempt such flicks from my fringe. My hairdo was a thing of beauty.

Later that night, I danced with my boy. But not in an inappropriate way. We danced to 'Nutbush City Limits' and we danced to the amazing song by Ray Parker Jr that had been the soundtrack to our first cinematic experience just a few months before. And as the evening drew to an end, he took me into the canteen to plant one last dry, quick peck on my lips.

And then it was over.

At the end of the summer holidays I left my little town, my little boyfriend and my little sheltered life. But I left with a wised-up heart, having felt both the joys and heartbreak that comes with falling in love—with someone who is not from the equine family.

7

PUBERTY BLUES IN A FLESH-COLOURED BRA

I never really thought too much about boobs as a kid. I mean, sure, I had seen them here and there, especially my mum's. But I was a skinny, lanky lass with a chest you could use as a spirit level—until I hit Year 5. And then something happened; something so mortifying, so humiliating, that even to this day I have been unable to erase it from my cerebral cortex.

I had been crook. Indeed, I must have been near death, because my mother actually presented me to our family doctor, Dr McIntosh, whose surgery was in a group of shops in the suburb of Hobartville. This is important to note, as there was a superior bakery nearby that sold the best doughnuts with thick pink icing, which was the only upside to a visit to the quack.

I sat on the table in Dr McIntosh's surgery, with my mum watching on as the doctor told me to remove my top and then applied a cold stethoscope to my back. He asked me to cough. Preoccupied by the prospect of pink doughnuts, I did as I was told, and the doctor listened intently. When I was done coughing and he was done listening, I turned to face him—and then he said something so embarrassing I wanted to die.

'You're getting a boob there,' he remarked casually, pointing to my left nipple with a pen.

'Oh, yes,' Mum chimed in. 'So she is!'

The conversation went on as if I were not in the room. I looked down at the offensive nipple and realised that it did look a little different. But was it normal to discuss it as if one was trading observations about the weather?

If I had known the phrase 'And let us never speak of this again', I would have uttered it. Though as it happened it would have been unnecessary, as we didn't speak of it again—at least, not for a long time.

Eventually my right nipple cottoned on to the surging hormones and made itself known. Then together they began to be backed by actual boob until it was fairly obvious what lay in store for me next.

When it comes to growing up and puberty, it seems to me there are two camps. I was in the first of these: the one that believes ignorance is bliss. I was not at all interested in turning into a woman and walked about with my shoulders hunched forward, trying to hide my growing chest. In the other camp were the girls who were positively delighted with their blooming bodies and wore their bras with pride.

So you can just imagine my delight when, one Saturday morning, Mum told me that we were going shopping to buy my first bra. I insisted that it was not yet required, but she was equally adamant that it was.

The bra shop was in a local mall frequented by people we knew. It had the butcher, the greengrocer and the bakery, and on a Saturday morning the joint was jumping.

Mum, seemingly oblivious to my cringing, stopped to chat with every friend and acquaintance she encountered, and to each one she stated the purpose of our mission.

'We're off to get her first bra!' she announced proudly, to admiring murmurs and covert glances at my chest.

Once she had ensured the entire town knew that I had boobs on the move, we headed for the Blue Bayou Boutique, where the true nightmare was about to unfold.

'Christine!' cried the saleswoman. 'How can I help you today?'

Mum explained that I needed my first bra, and they both practically shat themselves with excitement at the prospect.

The saleswoman—whom we shall henceforth refer to as Delvene, because she was a Delvene if ever I saw one—had a massive bust. I'm fairly certain that she was made of 100 per cent bosom, because it was impossible to see beyond her ample and heaving chest. At least I would be dealing with an expert, I consoled myself.

'Come on then,' Delvene barked at me. 'Give us a look.'

Did she seriously expect me to disrobe so she could gawk at my buds? I looked for some reassurance from my mother, but she was busy making sure everyone else in the shop knew why we were there.

Up until this point, I'd suffered a few humiliating experiences in my life. Getting stuck up a tree in front of a group of boys was pretty bad. Wetting my pants in the car while it was parked in the hot sun was not up there with my favourite recollections. Neither was performing 'Memories' from the musical *Cats* during the school talent quest. But this—this unfolding scenario—was the deadset winner.

Resigned to my fate, I removed my top and stood rigid as Delvene inspected my chest from all angles.

After several excruciatingly long minutes, she delivered her verdict. 'I think she's a 10A, Christine,' she pronounced.

Delvene bustled off, thankfully remembering to pull the curtain back across the changing room. I continued to stand there, looking at posters of ample-busted ladies draped over yachts and office desks wearing only matching bras and panties. Was this what I was supposed to do? Who were these women? Why were they so happy with their boobs?

Eventually Delvene and my mum reappeared, clutching a selection of elastic bands with scraps of fabric attached to them. These, apparently, were my bras. And so began a new round of torture as Delvene helped me into one wispy garment after another. Once I was 'fitted', she and Mum would both look at me critically, until one would convince the other that this was not the right one. The offending bra would be discarded onto the reject pile, and I was wrangled into the next contender.

Eventually they agreed on a simple flesh-coloured bra that did up at the front. Flesh-coloured was preferable to white, I learned, because it didn't show up the dirt as much. I looked at myself in the mirror, and then up at the glamazon lingerie models in the posters. I could see absolutely no correlation between me and them.

And that was how I acquired my first bra.

I didn't ever wear it, of course. It just sat in my drawer in all its beige glory. Sometimes I would pull it out and show my friends if they happened to be over for a play. It wasn't until I hit high school, where if you didn't wear a bra you were a complete deadshit, that my bra ever saw the light of day.

✳

If I had plenty of time to adjust to my first bra, periods, on the other hand, didn't give you any time to prepare.

When I was a lot younger, I would look at the tampons on Mum's dressing table and presume that they were rather large tablets. One day, I asked, 'Mum, what are these?' and she sat me down on her bed and gave it to me with both barrels.

When she was done, I literally staggered from the room, mortified, and swore to myself that that was never going to happen to me. How barbaric! How revolting! It all seemed so wrong, and even though Mum had been *very* thorough with her explanation, it still made no sense to me at all.

When, years later, Flo did actually come to town, Mum handed me a Modess and delivered a touching speech about how I was growing into a woman. To this very day, she still calls anything feminine hygiene-related a 'Modess'. Clearly the Modess marketing department of the day did a cracker of a job.

✳

I grew up in a fairly liberal household and I like to think I am a part of one now. But that's not to say I didn't suffer a few awkward moments when it came to explaining the facts of life to my son.

I was in the kitchen making dinner one day when Harry wandered in and demanded, totally out of the blue, 'Tell me the truth, Mum: have you ever sexed Dad?'

56

Well, I just about cut my finger off.

I told him to go to the lounge room and I would come and talk to him in a minute. And then I had a minor panic attack. I mean, the kid was seven and had already begun with the hard questions. I wasn't sure what to do. Should I just brush it off, make up some bullshit story and hope the whole thing would go away?

No, I knew I had to address it, so I poured myself a stiff vodka and tonic and sat down on the couch with Harry to have 'the talk'.

Big swig of vodka.

'So, darling, what do you think sexing is?'

'When you kiss and cuddle in bed,' he replied.

'Correct.' I told him.

There was a silence. I could tell he was waiting for me to say something more.

I took a big swig of vodka. I looked at him. He looked at me. I wanted to die.

I started to explain about falling in love and having funny feelings in your tummy about someone. By this stage I had a pleasant little buzz going on and was talking in circles. I was confusing myself. So I ripped off the band-aid, so to speak.

I actually used my fingers to symbolise a vagina and a penis and did the jabbing motion, like we did as an offensive gesture when I was in high school.

Harry just stared at me blank-faced. So then I used my hands to make a little tadpole swimming towards an egg, explaining that they joined up to make a tiny baby that grew inside the mummy's tummy until, after a long time, the baby was ready to come out.

'Where does it come out?' he enquired.

Big swig of vodka.

'It comes out through the mummy's vagina.'

'How?' he asked.

'With much difficulty,' I told him.

He seemed okay with it. Not once did he look like he wanted to run away. He said, 'So you and Dad have done this twice then . . .'

So I went on to tell him that when people love each other, sometimes they show their love for each other by doing it . . . you know . . . like, for fun.

It was this part that he found the most offensive. 'You do that for *fun?*'

By this stage I was onto my second vodka and I really wanted to say I did it because I was nagged to death by his father and really most of the time I would have preferred to watch *Chelsea Lately* over a bowl of Maggie Beer's ice-cream, but the romantic in me told him that it was a very special thing to do. (But you could not do it until you were married and even then you had to wait until you were thirty otherwise you went to jail for life.)

The birds and the bees. Puberty. Sex education. I acquired my knowledge of these subjects through a mixture of resources. I can recall going to the library in primary school with my parents for a very special presentation by some woman from the Department of Education. She gave us each a copy of *Where Did I Come From?* and we all read it together.

But I also learnt a lot about sex from watching documentaries where buffalos would be going at it hammer and tongs. Also from the local dogs, who could be spotted humping here and there because dogs were free to roam the streets back then, and desexing wasn't as widespread. I also learnt a lot about sex from Judy Blume, the author of such literary masterpieces as *Forever*, in which Katherine and Michael (and Michael's penis Ralph) end up doing it on the bedroom floor, before she dumps him for an older tennis instructor called Leo.

And that, my friends, is a real life lesson.

SMALL SCHOOL TALES

I asked writer Emily Toxward to share with me a few of her own memories about being a primary school kid in a small school. Here is her story.

I'm not the sharpest razor on the shelf, but what I lack in intelligence I make up for in sheer guts and determination, or in the words of three of my primary school teachers: 'Emily tries hard'.

From their over-seventies lifestyle villas, Miss Yeoman, Mr Connor and Mrs Curtis would happily tell you that nothing came easy to me as a kid. My gangly and uncoordinated limbs meant I was always last picked when it was soccer time and my inability to lose gracefully meant I once got an F for sportsmanship after throwing a cricket bat at the bowler in anger. This sort of anti-social behaviour is common at primary school, but it sticks out more when you attend a country school with a roll of twelve.

Sure there were years when a new family moved to the district and the number grew to fifteen, but for most of my primary school years there were a dozen kids aged from five to twelve years. The local community fundraised to buy an old Bedford school bus and it drove on windy and dusty roads to pick my sisters and me up from a cobweb-filled bus stop a few kilometres from our sheep and cattle farm. You learnt to hold in your vomit because Mrs Kennedy would stop for no one or nothing.

There were two things I nailed at primary school: trying really hard and crying. Not surprisingly, these things often went hand-in-hand. I vividly recall my first day of school because I had just got a new blue Annie schoolbag and Mum packed the first of my 2132 Vegemite and lettuce sandwiches. (Yes, the lettuce did go soggy and I always threw it out.)

I was an excruciatingly shy and sensitive child with thin white-blonde hair, chicken legs and the incredible ability to literally cry when I dropped a hat. School wasn't a foreign place to me because my sister was already there and I'd been to a few end-of-year prize-giving events where parents drank wine and then drove home with their kids sprawled out in the boot of the car in their sleeping bags.

You'd think having an older sister to show me the ropes would be an advantage; not so, because while I had no friends she had three or four and they had great pleasure in finding new ways to make me cry. The easiest way was to creep up behind me when I was taking a drink from the water fountain outside the library. It was often smattered in bird shit and shaped like a half circle and I was always nervous about putting my head in it.

The kicker with this fountain was that unlike today's water givers that have a set flow, there was an adjustable tap on the side that could be altered to alter the water pressure and flow. It was a bully's dream. I can't count the number of times someone would creep up behind me and twist the tap to full tilt, consequently sending water gushing up my nose and all over my Hypercolour t-shirt and red Ladybird cords.

Big sis wasn't the only one who did this to me; older boys seemed to find it hilarious over and over again, much like they did with teasing me about my Monday, Tuesday, Wednesday Thursday and Friday knickers, which I used to accidentally show them while sprawled on the mat. Looking back, that fountain was a rite of passage at my school and, despite numerous attempts by the local plumber to adjust the water pressure, the fountain continued to be a source of angst for some and of pleasure for others.

In fairness to my sister, she didn't always terrorise me; usually she'd do her best to avoid me, particularly when it came to games of T-ball or cricket. I'd usually end up being one of the last two kids left waiting to be picked, the other was a sickly asthmatic girl and no one wanted her to die on their watch. I was the next worse because, like a wonky supermarket trolley, I had no sense of direction and I ran slowly and awkwardly. At school cross-country events I'd always try to fake an illness because I got sick of coming last. Despite my long legs I was no athlete, and much to the amusement of my classmates I frequently tripped over fresh air.

At home all bets were off and my sister and I were quite good mates. Well, except when I stole her

Cabbage Patch Kid to play with. In retaliation, she'd beheaded one of my Barbie dolls and pinched me until I cried. But that's what sisters do; one minute you're playing nicely and the next you're calling each other horrible names and whispering death threats under your breath.

I recall one particularly traumatic day at school that made me realise it was never a good idea to turn your back on someone—a lesson I remember to this day. Me and my new short-back-and-sides hairdo—a result of mum's adherence to practicality—were quietly playing gutter ball all by ourselves on the tennis court when my sister came at me with a handful of worms from the garden.

Unlike me, she's never had to try too hard in life to be naturally good at things such as running, and so it didn't take her long to catch me. I let out a bloodcurdling scream because, while I've always been unafraid of large animals, anything that crawls, scuttles or slimes their way through life is a source of terror for me. My sister had the inside scoop on this and took great pleasure in showing off to her mates as she terrified me with worms.

Being the crier that I was, I burst into tears and soon a crowd of onlookers gathered to laugh at my ridiculously insane fear of these defenceless wrigglers. You see most of us were country kids and were used to throwing sheep shit at each other for fun, watching ewes give birth to lambs and hearing our dad's yell, 'You fucking stupid piece of shit dog—you've got shit for brains'. We weren't supposed to be petrified of worms; we were supposed to laugh in the face of them. I was never very good as being who I was supposed to be.

But it wasn't all wedgies and worms; there were plenty of fun times at my small country school, like a group of kids going over to the principal's house and watching David Attenborough videos on the TV in his lounge room. It got super awkward during humping scenes, but I chose these moments to indulge my nosey journo streak and gork at all the things in his house. He and his wife lived there courtesy of the Education Department, a trade-off for living in woop-woop and teaching a multitude of kids at various academic levels.

Another bonus was that once a week we got to leave school and head to Mrs Frew's house to learn how to cook. It was the first and last time I ever made hot cross buns and sausage-meat pasties.

In the classroom, coloured chalk was a treat, the overhead projector was a privilege not a right, and the large mat we sat on during story time was laden with crusty snot. Our old-fashioned wooden desks were tightly packed together and were the ones with heavy lids that were fun to smash down on your classmate's head. The ink holes in them made great rubbish bins and I used to stuff my pencil shavings down it in order to hasten my writing progress. I always wanted to be finished first and, as a result, my writing was illegible, but I didn't care as long as I could say I was done before anyone else. My competitive streak shined through at an early age.

My will to please was also strong back then and so I often resorted to cheating, especially when it came to maths—numbers and I don't gel. One afternoon after a particularly gruelling session of lunchtime tag, we sat down to complete a test. Thankfully I was sitting next to one of the class brains and I craned my neck to look at her answers. My left-handedness meant it wasn't hard for me to see the answers written by the person to the right of me. I must have been really struggling that day because I was a tad overzealous in my hovering and found myself just above her pencil. She got a fright, threw her hand up in shock and in the process jammed her HB up my schnozz, which started bleeding profusely. You would not freaking read about it. Oh, the shame of being caught cheating so blatantly was horrific. Understandably I was teased for being a big fat cheater and no one wanted to sit beside me. It took forever for that incident to be forgotten. Let's not forget that there was no escaping what I'd done, and I couldn't exactly go off and play with another bunch of kids because there were no other kids to play with.

When I was ten years old, my sister departed for an all-girls boarding school, my younger sibling had started school and the three kids who were my age left to travel into town to start Intermediate—a school in between primary and high school. Intermediate was where you learned to kiss, showed off your new bra, and used maths to figure out how much you loved someone.

It was also a place where firm friendships were made and bitchiness was rife. While my former schoolmates were practising pashing their arms and falling in love with a new boy every day, I was wearing elastic-waisted pants up to my chest, helping snotty-nosed six-year-olds tie their shoelaces, and playing the recorder. You should have seen me on that thing, all spittling and snuffling to hits such as 'You Are My Sunshine' and 'Yesterday'. My teacher Mrs Curtis played the piano, was two heads shorter than me, and always seemed to have coffee breath. (Now that I'm an adult and a mum to three, I get why every single grown-up I knew as a kid always had coffee or tea breath—it was to help them survive another day in the trenches.)

Mrs Curtis used to be a music teacher and so at the end of each year she'd relive her youth and make us put on a musical for our parents. Guess who was the lead two years running? Damn straight bitches. Me and all my recorder geekiness. Sure it was by default as I was the only one left in my year, but I'll take it.

For my final year at primary school she chose *The Pied Piper of Hamelin* and I was to be the Piper. I spent every spare second I had learning my lines, singing to my pet lamb Tinkerbell and practising my recorder in front of Rascal and Kitty Cat, our two farm cats who took pleasure in placing half-eaten rabbits under my bed. I was horrendously out of tune and to this day I can't sing a note to save myself, but that doesn't stop me from belting out a few Tiffany and Bananarama songs when they come on the radio in the car. I remember feeling slightly embarrassed singing on stage, but Mrs Curtis made me feel like I was an opera singer. If I could, I'd apologise to each and every parent for putting them through such an ordeal. Mind you, they were probably half cut on goon so won't remember it anyway.

Looking back I don't think going to such a tiny school did me any harm; well, except when it came to boys. I was captain clueless about the opposite sex because I had no brothers, went to a primary school with only five of them, and was then shipped to an all-girls boarding school until I was sixteen. Come to think of it I did bloody well to find one that would marry me, but then again I always did try very hard.

Visit Emily's blog @ havealaughonme.com.

—8—

SCHOOL CAMP: CLOGS, CORDIAL AND CULTURE

Camps always loomed large on the school calendar, though the reality very rarely lived up to the promise. When I recall the school camps I attended, one in particular always springs to mind . . .

We were on an 'adventure' camp. At least, it was called an 'adventure' camp, but really it was more like a povvo camp for the privileged. I was going to a posh private school by then and, along with a dozen others, we were to spend a week living in the bush, testing our survival skills. This involved variety of mind-numbingly boring activities, such as erecting tents, building fire and eating really disgusting food that came in packages. Food like Deb mashed potato and sliced Spam that was warmed up in a dodgy-looking pan. Is it any wonder that I abhor camping to this day?

As if the food wasn't bad enough, there were the physical activities designed to test our endurance and strength and to promote teamwork. Naturally, it was one of these activities that saw my self-esteem plummet, my social standing collapse and my humiliation levels rise to heights never seen before.

It all began with this bastard fucking obstacle course that we had to complete. And, oh yes, there was mud and a light sprinkle of rain that we would just have to suck up, because we were not the special snowflakes that we thought we were.

So I started the course. Jumped in ditches, swung across a creek, ran up a hill, ran back down the hill, hauled my arse over a wall, crawled under a menacing layer of barbed-wire fencing and navigated my way through a maze of tyres while crawling through the mud.

And it was at this point that it all went pear-shaped. And being pear-shaped was the whole problem, as my newly acquired hips just didn't want to go through that first tyre.

My arms went through easily enough, followed by my head and shoulders. But then either the tyre magically shrank five centimetres or my hips suddenly exploded in deference to my impending womanhood. Either way, I was wedged in tight. There was no going forward, and no going back.

I am hysterical by nature, so rather than trying calmly to extricate myself, I wriggled and thrashed around in a desperate attempt to shake myself free. Needless to say, my increasingly frantic motions had the opposite effect. If anything, I was now wedged tighter.

Fuckety fuckety fuck!

Exhausted, both mentally and physically, I lay there. The rain grew heavier. I shut my eyes.

Eventually the girl doing the course behind me caught up and, correctly assessing my sticky (as in stuck) situation, alerted the authorities. Loudly. This, of course, drew a crowd.

Now, I can honestly say that teenage girls are bitches. Someone produced a camera (thank GOD there were no iPhones and Facebook back then) and started snapping away as if I was some sort of freak show. By this point I was screaming like a banshee at the girl with the camera to stop. And you can guess what effect swelling with rage had on my predicament.

The teachers went completely mental, shouting at everyone to calm down while clearly panicking as they wondered how the fuck they were going to explain to my parents that I now came with a spare.

The rest of the audience was relocated back to the main camp while the teachers tried to work out the physics required to free me. It took a very long time, but they finally managed to dig out the part of the tyre that was buried in the mud and pull me up to a standing position—still with the tyre around my hips.

The teachers were trying to decide the best way to cut through rubber when I realised that my spare tyre seemed a little looser.

Gingerly, gingerly, gingerly, the teachers rotated the tyre over my gargantuan hips and down to the ground.

I stepped out. I was free! I told my saviours that, after the stress of my ordeal, I wanted to go home. They replied, 'Tough luck.' I started to cry.

Then we made our way back to the main camp, where I was greeted with a welcome normally reserved for astronauts returning from a space mission. I quickly found the photographer and told her what I thought of her. She promised to give me the photos once she'd had the film developed and swore she would show no one.

Which was complete bullshit, as the photos were subsequently used in a slide show presented to the rest of the year level, who had gone on different camps. IT WAS THE FIRST SLIDE. That girl is lucky I am so nice, as I am very tempted to write her name right here on this page, so everyone can know what a double-crossing bitch she is. But I won't.

But we'd better move on quickly before I change my mind.

Another popular school trip back then, and one that is still popular now, was the Canberra/Snowy Mountains haul. Accompanied by the Year 5 and 6 teachers, we travelled by bus from the outskirts of Sydney and down the Hume Highway to Goulburn. Here we stopped so the bus driver could have a smoke and we could run madly around the park in the middle of town. In this we were encouraged by the teachers, who hoped that this burst of physical exertion would tire us out sufficiently that we would shut the fuck up for the rest of the trip.

I recall being very excited as we crossed the border into the Australian Capital Territory. What a novel idea! One second you were in New South Wales, the next you were in a whole new world. A world of wide, clean streets and signs pointing out the many attractions that Canberra has to offer.

We took in the sights of Cockington Green, a miniature village created in 1979 by a gentleman named Doug. Its purpose? Well, I am not really sure of its educational merit, but it did have a free barbeque area, if you felt like cooking a steak.

Next we visited Parliament House, which was about as interesting to a group of eleven-year-olds as you would assume. We learnt why our capital ended up smack bang in the middle of nowhere. (Because Sydney and Melbourne could not get their shit together and agree which should be the capital city, so they created a new city between the two.) Meanwhile, construction was underway on the *real* Parliament House. The government-appointed tour guide could not get us enthused about any of it.

Bob Hawke was the prime minister at the time. 'Advance Australia Fair' had just been voted the country's national anthem and, despite the hues on our flag, our national colours had just been announced as green and gold. These were years of great change. Medicare was established. The Australian dollar was floated. We had won the America's Cup. Sir Ninian Stephen formally handed the title deeds to Uluru back to the traditional landowners. But none of these significant milestones in our nation's history could compare to the excitement of discovering that there was a vending machine at Parliament House.

Then we were herded back onto the bus. Next stop: Cooma, a bitterly cold town where we would spend the night in large dormitories run by a local religious cult that was keen to cash in on the passing school-excursion trade. The number-one tourist attraction at the time was a shop that sold traditional Dutch clogs. While we hadn't been able to muster any enthusiasm during our tour of Parliament House, this little shop of clogs was a huge hit. We learnt the history of clogs and were treated to an excellent demonstration of how they were carved from a single block of wood. Finally, we were let loose in the gift shop. I recall the glee with which I bought a key ring for my mother that had a miniature clog hanging from it.

That evening at the cult hotel, we were given dinner along with jugs of green cordial. Of course, no one slept that night after the heady mix of clogs and cordial and the anticipation of seeing snow the next day.

As we drove out of Cooma, the bus driver made a lame attempt to interest us in the Snowy Mountains Hydro-Electric Scheme, but we weren't having a bar of it; we were too busy competing to be the first person to spy a snow-covered peak.

'I see it!' someone squawked and the bus erupted into cheers.

As we drew closer to our destination, snow began to appear in little clumps by the side of the road. We arrived at a place called Dead Horse Gap, which was a nod to all the brumbies that had frozen to death over the years. The doors of the bus were opened and a group of tired and cranky teachers basically told us to go and knock ourselves out.

Now, we were a group of Western Sydney kids, most of whom had never seen snow before. For some reason—most likely an excess of high spirits, exhaustion and green cordial, the snow ignited something feral in us. The boys basically beat the shit out of each other in the snow, while the girls ran shrieking as a flurry of snowballs rained down on us. Here is a little something about snowballs: when packed down very hard, they have very little give. Like none at all. You might as well be throwing a brick at someone.

After an hour, one of the teachers appeared at the door of the bus and yelled that our time was up. The lads made sure that they left as much yellow snow as possible, and we drove away from Dead Horse Gap nursing a plethora of injuries.

So . . . that was our trip to the snow.

The bus travelled back to Canberra, where, because our teachers had not self-flagellated enough on this trip, we visited the art gallery. Now, having taken groups of students to art galleries myself, I know that kids have zero interest in looking at paintings and sculptures—unless the subjects are naked. Naked art is like gold.

When you find a picture of a nude, you immediately alert your fellow pupils. You then gather around it to laugh and point. This will cause your teacher to come running in from another room and scold you all in a very vicious whisper.

You disperse, still giggling. Then one of you happens upon a huge bronze statue of a naked lady. So you alert your fellow pupils—and so on and so forth until your teacher cracks the shits and you leave.

Has every primary school kid on the east coast of Australia done a similar camp? Canberra? Clog factory? Dead Horse Gap?

From what I can tell, the Canberra/Snowy Mountains trip is a rite of passage, as generations of teachers attempt to introduce students to our political system and our artistic heritage. Thank God for clogs and penises, I say!

—9—

THE SMELL OF TEEN SPIRIT

At the age of twelve, I was sent off to a posh boarding school in the northern suburbs of Sydney to be turned into a well-rounded, intelligent, thoughtful global citizen, capable of doing anything I put my mind to because I am woman, hear me roar.

Twelve is a very young age to be let loose on the world, which was effectively what happened. Thirty girls from around Australia were thrown together in a dormitory and told to play nice. Add one geriatric old bag, the housemistress, whose accommodation was at the furthest point of the building, and hey—what could possibly go wrong?

The boarding house was an old Federation number with worn carpets and the smell of teen spirit. When you entered the foyer, the housemistress's apartment was to the left. On the right was a big staircase, which led up to a long hall. At the end of the hall

75

there was a room the size of a football field. This was divided into cubicles, each one housing four beds.

Next to your bed, you had a small chest of drawers topped with a mirror and next to that, a small hanging space.

The whole place smacked of neglect and was not exactly the sort of place that could be described as a lovely home away from home. I recall my mum unpacking all my belongings, making up my bed and then getting the hell out of there. I sat on the bed and ate an entire jar of green olives, watching as the three girls who were to share my cubicle came in one by one with their parents and their gear. Finally, it was just the four of us, sitting on our freshly made beds, looking at each other.

One girl started crying and the rest of us went over and comforted her. And then we heard other little whimpers floating up over the cheap partitions. Soon the whole room was awash with tears.

My six-year stint at boarding school taught me more about life than any part of the actual curriculum ever did. These years taught me to be rat-cunning, to question the establishment, to defy authority and to save my own arse.

I will not go into all of the dreadful things the class of '91 got up to, because some of you might actually have daughters at boarding school right this minute, and I fear that with the advances in technology since my day, things might have got even worse. But I will share with you my highlights reel—or should that be lowlights reel?—to give you a sense of what I took away from the experience . . .

*

A popular weekend activity among one group was to take the train to nearby Chatswood, a large shopping precinct only a few stops away. The purpose of the expedition was shoplifting. And when I say shoplifting, I don't mean nicking a red frog from the counter of the local milk bar; I'm talking about expensive items that the boarders would then on-sell to the daygirls at a reduced rate. Levi's jeans, Doc Martens, dresses—everything was fair game. One girl in particular, a doctor's daughter from a country town near the Queensland border, was a kleptomaniacal genius. If it wasn't nailed down, she shoved it up her top. They grew so practised at it that eventually they began to take requests and stole to order.

For some reason—perhaps still wary after my long-ago ladybird-hairclip spree—I never got involved in this racket. I certainly played my part when it came to other shenanigans, though.

My first suspension was in Year 8. It was for something that, if you ask me, should have seen me hailed for showing early signs of entrepreneurial excellence, not derided as a common thief. You see, the Christian group in the school, known as the Crusaders, was going to hold a dance to raise money for some worthy cause (I can't remember what). One day, I happened to walk past the table they had set up to sell tickets at $5 a throw.

Now this dance was to be held in conjunction with the local boys school, so I knew that there would be much interest in attending, because . . . BOYS. So I waited until the two girls at the table were distracted, then I slunk over and swiped a handful of tickets.

By lunchtime, word had got around that one of the Year 8 girls (that would be me) was selling tickets to the hot event for half-price. I sold out of tickets in no time, and was just contemplating how I could get my hands on some more when I was approached by a teacher, who told me that the headmistress would like to see me.

BUSTED!

Apparently, tales of my business prowess had reached the ears of some meddling do-gooder, who had turned me in.

I found the headmistress—a woman who looked uncannily like a Border Leicester sheep, if you can picture that—sat behind her desk, nostrils flared so wide you could make out the shape of her brain.

'Sit down,' she thundered.

So I sat, and confessed all.

Then followed a solid thirty minutes' berating: I was a disappointment; I was wicked; I was no better than a common thief. By rights I should be expelled on the spot.

Then the door opened and in walked my mum. To be honest, I think she was more scared than me. The headmistress gave her a toned-down version of the lecture she had given me, and then I was sent home for five days to have a good think about what I had done.

On the way home, Mum was a bit cross with me, but not as much as I'd feared. When we got home she rang my dad and told him what I'd done, and I listened from the next room as they laughed about my business acumen.

*

I was suspended for the second time the following year. There was nothing clever or entrepreneurial about my crime this time; it was more of a straight snatch-and-grab.

Oh Lord, forgive me, because indeed I did sin. I stole in your house.

I stole the contents of the chapel plate.

Okay, so in my defence Levi's had just brought out a range of white jeans. WHITE LEVI'S! I needed them in my life.

On the day of my crime there had been a special collection so that the Crusaders could buy bicycles for Nepalese orphans. By some twist of fate, I had been put in charge of counting the collection, along with another girl whom I *thought* was my friend.

The bowls were heavy with coins and the final tally amounted to several hundred dollars. Well, several hundred dollars minus the thirty bucks that ended up in my pocket.

Later, as I was treating my mates to Paddle Pops from the canteen, a Year 12 girl approached with a message: I was to report to the office immediately.

BUSTED!

So off I went to that old familiar place. Though there had been some changes, I noticed, as I sat outside the headmistress's office; they had changed the art around.

The office door opened and out walked my 'friend'. HER NAME WAS ANNABELLE KELLY.

God, it feels good to get that out. You might know her; she's now an architect up on the north coast of New South Wales.

About the changes I mentioned; it wasn't only the art. At the beginning of the school year, we were introduced to a new head-mistress, as the older one had retired. But the change wasn't too drastic. This new headmistress was also sheep-like in appearance, which is to say that she didn't have hair—she had wool.

They must have had a handbook, these headmistresses, on how to deal with delinquents, for she delivered nearly the same speech as her predecessor, almost word perfect.

'Why shouldn't I expel you right now?' she asked me.

So I told her that my parents would be super pissed off (though not in those exact words).

Then—because history was clearly repeating—the door opened and in walked my mother.

Addressing the headmistress, she lamented the fact that they were meeting each other for the first time under such dreadful circumstances, and then proceeded to charm the pants suit off the woman. She handed over a large cheque for the building fund and whisked me off for a week at home.

This time, however, the mood at home was less jovial than it had been during my last forced break. I actually had to do non-fun stuff, like sort out old files in my stepfather's office. It wasn't even in the office. It was a cold, stinky basement.

Plus my mum was pulling out the old 'no speakies' punishment—aka the silent treatment—which is still very effective in this modern day. And when she did talk, it was to deliver long, sad lectures on the subject of disappointment. Ah, that word: *disappointed*. The worst one a parent can use.

I had learnt my lesson.

Thou shall not steal.

When I returned to school, I discovered that my friends had decided they didn't want me to get expelled—the prospect of which was only the puff of a ciggie away—so from then on each time I was the main suspect for a crime, one of them took the fall.

That was the thing about growing up in a small group of girls. We stuck together through thick and thin. We knew each other in a way that no one else ever will and it is a bond that has lasted. While time and geography have scattered us far and wide, that closeness and camaraderie has endured. I was lucky to have encountered such a great group of gals, for it is those school years that truly shape who you ultimately turn out to be. I am grateful not to be in jail. I am grateful that my parents persisted with me despite my evil ways. I am grateful that social media didn't exist at that time. And, in a way, I am even grateful to Annabelle Kelly, that fucking nark. Most of the notorious criminals in the world started their careers as petty thieves—but I turned out to be a mummy blogger. The only thing I steal these days are an extra Tim Tam when I think no one is looking.

MIND YOUR P'S AND Q'S

Here's a story that a friend shared with me about her primary school days:

> I went to an all-girls' school—gloves, hats, ribbons and regulation underpants were the order of the day. Non-compliance with outerwear was fairly easy to spot . . . but woe betide anyone who thought underwear might be different. The PE teacher also acted undercover as the underpants compliance officer and a mere flash of pink or bloom of floral peeking defiantly from gym gear would be enough to be sent to the office for a second-hand pair of grey, high-waisted cottontails.
>
> Our school principal was a spinster in her eighties. As the school's founder, she was untouchable in her role and refused to retire

despite her advanced age and declining faculties. Not only was she a living relic with outmoded ideas of what a good girl should be—she also had a rather elevated view of herself and her position. Literally. She'd sit on the balcony outside her second storey office on a throne-like chair and survey all beneath her. When she bought a new fridge for the tuckshop, we all had to line up across the playground, climb the stairs and file past her to say thank you. As there were hundreds of us, this took quite a while and a number of girls fainted in the sun as if overcome with devotion.

—PART TWO—

JOINING THE CIRCUS

—10—

NOT MY MONKEYS

You know that old Polish proverb, 'Not my monkey, not my circus'? Well, that's the opposite of what you're faced with if you choose a career in primary school teaching. Suddenly you are the ringmaster of the most crazy circus of all.

A disturbing number of people think teachers have it easy, what with the short hours and the long holidays, but the reality is that teachers slog away for hours behind the scenes, require the patience of ten saints, must have a working knowledge of psychology and a mind as sharp as a bear trap.

My first realisation that teaching was no skip through the park came when I had a kindergarten class full of children who, at the beginning of the year, were all unable to do any of the following:

- Tie their shoes.
- Use scissors.
- Stand in a line.
- Open a lunchbox.
- Work a zip.

- Write their names without it being backwards.
- Remain awake after lunchtime.

But, geezers, they were adorable. Even when the nit infestation hit.

Still, it was very taxing, and being a rookie teacher, I had plenty to learn that was not covered in any of my university lectures.

Let me take you through one scenario that I survived.

As Easter drew close, I had decided to do a fun craft activity and follow it up with a little Easter egg hunt, which would then turn into a little maths lesson about counting. Seems straightforward enough, right?

I ran off the stencil, which was the template of an Easter basket, and I wrote each child's name on his or her basket (thereby saving us at least an hour). The kids were then instructed to colour in the basket, which took forever, and then cut them out. It was then I discovered that not one child in the class was capable of using a pair of scissors.

So I sat at my desk while the kids lined up with their baskets, and I cut out like a motherfucker. When I'd finished cutting, I had to fold along the dotted lines, and then use my stapler to fix the resulting basket into place. I had to do this thirty-one times.

Thirty-one times.

I was at my wits' end. What educational purpose did any of this serve, apart from me having a small breakdown?

My lesson plan was thrown out the window as the baskets took shape. After I had made thirty-one baskets, we wandered outside to find a large, stray dog of mixed breed scoffing down the tiny Easter eggs, foil and all.

Cue mass hysteria. The dog fled and I surveyed the carnage. A couple of eggs had been spared, but not enough for everyone.

I threw my hands in the air and took the crying mob back inside, where I told them that they could have free play for the rest of the day. 'Free play' is code for 'Do whatever the fuck you want'. Which means destroy the classroom. But I didn't care. I was over it.

*

Classroom management is not an easy thing to get your head around. If you expect the unexpected at every turn, you will be better equipped to survive the school day. Like, if one of the kids in your classroom turns green, stands up and announces that they don't feel particularly well, then empties the contents of their stomach and bowels simultaneously, you can pretty much assume that you are on the beginning of a gastro highway that will, in a very short time, wipe our your entire class, and end with you succumbing to it yourself.

Classroom management is about trying to make your class aware that you are waiting for their attention by standing at the front with your arms crossed, saying nothing but just waiting and waiting and waiting until one kid realises that you are pulling the old 'I will just wait until you notice that I am waiting for you all to shut up' move and starts letting his fellow pupils know that there might be a hell of an explosion if they don't acknowledge that I am playing the waiting game.

Classroom management means being aware of the worst-case scenario for every part of your day. What if the slide projector doesn't work? What if the mums who promised to come and do reading groups don't show up? What if the strange mark on that kid's arm is actually a ringworm?

Classroom management is about using another tried and true method of gaining the class's attention: CLAP. CLAP.

CLAP-CLAP-CLAP. Do it now, as you read this book, and if there is a primary school kid within hearing distance, I bet you will hear them clap it back to you. It is ingrained in them from the age of six.

There are some teachers who are experienced guns at classroom management, who could tell you what they were planning on teaching a month out, to the minute, and which outcomes they will be focusing on from the syllabus. These are the teachers who, when you turn up to their classrooms, have the students all doing small group work in hushed tones while she or he wanders around, all nice and in control.

You see, the thing is, if kids sniff out a weakness, they will exploit it until the teacher has to flee the classroom in tears. But teachers, being humans (yes, really), are all different, and we have different ideas of what we think is acceptable behaviour.

You have to hand it to those teachers who run their classroom like the circus. Their room looks like a craft cupboard has exploded. Their desks are littered with empty coffee cups. The kids might be sitting on the floor finger-knitting while listening to Mozart. These teachers are usually dressed from head to toe in floaty garments bought at Tree of Life. They have a high tolerance for noise and chaos. One of my kid's teachers actually carried a turtle in her pocket. These teachers are golden.

I once worked with a teacher whose passion was art, and together he and his class would create amazing artworks. He would then go into his classroom every weekend to spend time mounting the kids' artworks onto carefully cut card, before laminating them and putting them up on display, so the kids would get a thrill when they came in on Monday morning.

And then there was the teacher who taught dance. She would spend hours and hours choreographing routines and teaching them to the kids in her group. She also made their costumes herself and spent her own time and money making sure that her dance group got to perform at several concerts, thus giving them a sense of pride, accomplishment and confidence.

What do Sheryl Crow, Billy Crystal and J.K. Rowling have in common? They all started out as primary school teachers.

Before Gene Simmons put together a little musical group called KISS, he taught sixth grade at a New York public school, before he was fired (allegedly for a bit of freestyling with the curriculum, replacing the works of Shakespeare with the more popular option of Spider-Man comics).

If you attended Litchfield Prep in Connecticut back in the day, your maths teacher might have been Art Garfunkel.

And Mr Sumner, a teacher from Cramlington, England, is quoted as saying, 'One of the most important jobs in the planet is to teach children. Our entire future depends on children being educated.'

Wise words indeed . . . STING!

Famous or not, primary school teachers play one of the most important roles in modern society, and we neither respect them nor pay them enough.

According to a 2014 OECD survey, the best place to be a primary school teacher in terms of salary and workload is the tiny country of Luxembourg, where the average starting salary of a qualified primary teacher comes in at US$52,000 compared to Australia's US$34,664.

Interestingly, Luxembourg also has one of the highest literacy rates in the world, and consumes more alcohol per head than any other European country. So the place is full of smart, well-paid, slightly pissed people. Go Luxembourg!

And speaking of wages and conditions, this brings me to a subject that a lot of parents find irritating, but I for one fully support: the teachers strike.

As a kid, I loved a teachers strike. Mum would cross herself as she went out to work, leaving my brother, sister and me to build forts out of the couch cushions and feast on the cooking chocolate that she used to hide on the top of the fridge.

These days, when a strike is called, I hear other parents crack the shits, complaining that teachers are selfish, and it takes every fibre of my being not to unleash a tirade of shame on those whingers. For teachers, a strike usually represents a desperate last-ditch effort to win some miniscule change to wages or conditions.

The other thing that must be considered is the amount of extra time our teachers must spend trying to keep up with technology. When I was a chalkie, we literally relied on chalk and a blackboard to deliver our lessons. Four classrooms shared a fancy little gadget called an overhead projector. These days, it's all smartboards, personal tablets, apps and anything else that is shiny. These are invariably full of razzle-dazzle, but first you need to learn how to work the darn things. So you need to go to workshops, many of which eat into your weekends and your evenings. But for the dedicated teacher, it is all a part of the job.

★

The great Maya Angelou once said, 'People will forget what you said, people will forget what you did, but people will never forget how you made them feel,' and this is certainly true of a great teacher. I remember beaming when getting a merit certificate, watching my teacher as she clapped me onto that stage. These poignant memories stick with you, and those feelings never really ever go away. You think about it. Who was your favourite teacher? I'll bet you can still remember their name.

Oh, don't get me wrong! I also recall a time in Year 1 being ordered out into the corridor for ten minutes due to my incessant chatter. It was, at the time, the most shameful thing that had ever happened to me. I remember standing outside the classroom wailing, thinking about how I had let my teacher down, sure that Mum would find out and would forbid me watch *The Wonderful World of Disney* on Sunday night.

After a while, the teacher stuck her head out into the corridor to check on me. She was so horrified to see how distraught I was that she raced over and hugged me until my tears had dried. She told me not to worry, and that everything was fine. I had just talked too much, that's all.

She made me feel better. That is a big deal for a seven-year-old drama queen. I went back into the classroom, and she winked at me as I took my place on the floor. That wink has stayed with me to this very day. And I remembered it, remembered the impact it had on me, as I went on to take my place behind the teacher's desk and became the ringmaster of my own circus.

A TRUE STORY

This is a true story (or so a friend tells me), proving how fascinating the mind of a six year old is. They think so logically.

A teacher was reading the story of the 'Three Little Pigs' to her class. She came to the part of the story where first pig was trying to gather the building materials for his home. She read: 'And so the pig went up to the man with the wheelbarrow full of straw and said: "Pardon me, sir, but may I have some of that straw to build my house?"'

The teacher paused then asked the class: 'And what do you think the man said?'

One little boy raised his hand and said very matter-of-factly: 'I think the man would have said . . . "Well, fuck me!! A talking pig!"'

The teacher had to leave the room.

—II—

WHO'S WHO IN THE STAFFROOM

When I began my (rather short-lived) teaching career, people would quite often give me shit about what was perceived to be rather cushy employment conditions. It's a common belief that teachers work from 9 am till 3 pm, five days a week, in ten-week blocks. And that you spend the rest of your time travelling the world in private jets, taking time out from cruising the Caribbean only to mix it with the high rollers at the casino in Monte Carlo.

I must admit that, at the time, the thought of this lifestyle was appealing.

The truth, you'll be surprised to learn, was a far cry from the fantasy.

The truth was that I got to school at 7.30 am and left at 5 pm if I was lucky. My holidays were spent recovering from noise pollution. And the money? Well, let's just say that teachers earn every cent. But as in every profession, there are good practitioners, average ones, and those who just should not be there. In your typical staffroom, you will probably find a mix of all three practitioners. And in your typical staffroom, you can categorise teachers into some basic stereotypes. (And YES, I know I am generalising, but we're just having fun here, okay?) So, sit up straight, eyes to the front, hands to yourself, and let us begin . . .

THE PRINCIPAL

The principal of the school inevitably determines the culture of the school—so you really want to get a good one. In days gone by, the principal was someone to be feared, for he (and it was most often a 'he') was the keeper of the cane and had the uncanny ability to reduce grown teachers to tears by the mere raising of an eyebrow . . . followed by a barrage of abuse.

There are still principals like that. I once worked under a principal who walked around with her head firmly inserted up her generous rectum. When presented with a wayward child, she had no hesitation in putting her face right up against the perpetrator's and, nostrils flaring, delivering a spray worthy of an Oscar. The ironic thing was that, other than this, she was a woman of few words.

Principals these days are different; well, the ones I've encountered, anyway. No longer do they hold themselves aloof, cloistered in their office. Instead they can be found wandering the school grounds, mixing with crowds of kids and parents. They know the name of every child, no matter how large the school community is. The effective modern principal is a diplomat, politician and wise counsellor.

There is a common theory that principals are just kids who never really grew up, but that's hardly the case. Well, hardly ever . . .

Years after I left primary school, I heard something about the principal that is probably just an urban myth—but is still too good not to share. One afternoon, the mother of one of my friends was wheeling her shopping trolley through the car park at the local shops when she saw the principal's car. The odd thing was that even though the car was unoccupied, it appeared to be moving.

Puzzled, she approached the car and peered in the window— and you can just imagine her face when she realised that our school principal, that pillar of society, that community leader, that personification of all things proper, was right then on the receiving end of a very vigorous blow job, performed by one of the school mums!

I suppose that principals, despite all their power, are just people after all.

And you know what they say. Behind (or should that be in front of?) every great leader is a . . .

DOOR BITCH

Sometimes known as the administrative officer, the door bitch is easily the most powerful person in the school community. Mark my words, people! This is very important information that I am about to bestow. Read and learn.

One hundred per cent of office ladies (as they are also called) are, as their moniker suggests, ladies. In smaller schools you might have a part-time office lady and in larger schools you can quite often see three. When there is more than one, it is inevitable that there will be a 'good cop' and a 'bad cop', and it is crucial to identify who is who.

Your good cop will be the one who acknowledges you when you arrive at the counter of the school office. Quite often greeting you with a beaming smile, she will enquire after your wellbeing and actually listen to the answer. If you have indeed not been well, she will offer her sympathy and maybe even suggest a remedy. She will have the answer to your enquiry without needing to go and check with someone from the staffroom. She will have the note you require in her left hand and she will make allowances for the fact that you are one of 'those busy, disorganised mums' without making you feel bad about it.

The bad cop is her polar opposite. She will ignore you for as long as she feels like it, before glancing up at you for a millisecond, then continuing her work as if she hadn't seen you. After some time, she will rise from her chair to go and make a cup of tea.

On her return, she will look at you in surprise and say something like, 'Oh, I didn't see you there . . .'

You will then ask her a question, or put in a request to, say, take your kid out of school for a specialist appointment and she will roll her eyes theatrically so that you understand exactly how much of a pain in the arse you are.

Then, after a lot of pencil grabbing, heavy sighing and paper shuffling, she will say something inaudible before disappearing down the hall, leaving you wondering whether she is in fact going to return.

The thing about the bad cop is that she essentially runs the school. She is keeper of the keys, the person with the power to decide if you can make an appointment with the principal. She is the one who calls and leaves messages on your phone like:

'This is Mrs Drivelguts from Snarly Guts Primary School. Call me back urgently!'

The good cop would leave the following message: 'This is Mrs Smiley from Happy Land Primary School. EVERYTHING IS FINE! I REPEAT, EVERYTHING IS FINE! YOUR KIDS ARE OKAY! I just need to check whether your son can go on the excursion today, because we didn't get a note back from you.'

It doesn't matter which variety of door bitch guards your school, it is in your best interests to be very, very nice to them.

THE GROUNDSMAN

The groundsman is generally a man of few words, but he doesn't need them. What is important is his ability to fix anything and everything with little more than duct tape and pipe cleaners. The uncanny thing is that while sometimes he seems to be everywhere at once, when something dramatic happens, like the toilet block exploding, he is nowhere to be found.

He lives in a little cupboard near the assembly hall and is forever tinkering with the lawnmower.

THE OLD TEACHER

Literally a dying breed, old teachers have taught through so many changes of government that they don't even care who the Minister of Education actually is anymore. They have seen phonics come in, go out, come in, go out and then come in, and the difference it has made to their teaching methods is diddly-squat.

They enjoy a cuppa and a biscuit for their morning tea. They have a tuna sandwich for lunch with a piece of fruit. They fear no child. They fear no parent. They are so consistent in their method you might start to suspect they could actually teach the curriculum in their sleep. They are respected by their fellow teachers and have paid their dues, meaning that they are no longer expected to take choir, dance group or any other extra assignments.

THE NEW TEACHER

Fresh-faced and fervent, the new teacher turns up on their first day of school, ready to change lives. With their heads full of theory, they quickly discover that classroom management is key if any quality teaching is to take place. They spend the first half of the year 'managing' students' behaviour and the second half of the year questioning their career choice. They have seen *Dead Poets Society* far too many times.

THE TEACHER WHO COULD NOT GIVE A FUCK

Cruising into school with a hangover five minutes before the bell rings, this type of teacher is only there for the paycheque. If you have one of these teachers educating your kid, expect little and you will never be disappointed.

THE JOCK

The young, attractive male teacher who young boys look up to and horny mothers want to bone, the jock is in charge of sports—as long as it's 'boys' sports, such as cricket and football. For some reason, even when not engaged in any sporting activity, this teacher is forever ensconced in sports clothes, apart from when there are official public duties, when he will wear a short-sleeved shirt. They are ageless, these jocks. If you went back to your own primary school right now, you'd see what I mean. He will still be there, whistle in hand.

THE LIBRARIAN

Her name is always Helen and her hair is mousy brown. Helen will hunt you down all over the playground when you borrow a copy of *The Discontented Pony* and fail to return it over the course of a whole school year. She will send home notes. She is like a Literary Terminator when it comes to persistence. Eventually your mum will crack the shits and make you empty your St George Dragon piggy bank and pay her the stupid $4.50 so she will shut the fuck up. Or so I believe.

THE SUBSTITUTE

The substitute teacher doesn't care about you. They truly do not. They are just there for the cash. A glorified babysitter in many cases. They are just there because the deputy principal called them early in the morning as one of the teachers has fallen foul of the latest plague to sweep through the school. For kids, a day with a substitute teacher is heaven, because there is a high chance that you will get to watch movies all day.

THE PRAC TEACHER

The polar opposite of a substitute teacher, the prac teacher is dead keen to display all of her learning that, before now, had taken place in lecture halls. She is more likely to be educated in the latest teaching methods and you may find yourself doing unusual things in class, like yoga and meditation.

THE DEPUTY PRINCIPAL

The deputy principal is perhaps the hardest working person in the school.

The deputy principal is a bit like the deputy prime minister. They do a hell of a lot of the work for very little glory. They are often required to attend meetings to gather information about forthcoming curriculum changes, or learn how to integrate teachers with special needs, or develop a better arts program using pinecones, or contribute to think tanks considering the development of mental computation in kindergarten.

They deal with the discipline of seriously wayward children, including making uncomfortable phone calls to the parents of these juvenile delinquents.

The deputy principal is the only one who can actually find the groundsman when a brown snake needs to be removed from the library.

The DP is an integral part of any ceremony. She or he is the person who stands at the front during the assembly, pleading with the kids to calm the fuck down, before introducing the principal, who then goes on to give some droning speech about community service and its importance, followed by the class act, which is most likely to be a Year 2 class singing 'My Favourite Things'.

The DP is there to greet any important visitors to the school, escorting them to the principal's office before running around madly, making sure that the flag is raised and the audiovisual equipment is primed to break down a mere four seconds into the presentation.

It is a tough gig, but they'll stick it out until they get that magic call from the Department of Education, offering them a school of their own to govern.

And then they are out of there without a backward glance.

So in conclusion, apart from the teacher who doesn't give a fuck, the staff of your local school work hard—damn hard. And for those who maintain that teachers are only in it for the holidays, well, you deserve a detention. After all, they also have to put up with you—and you might be one of those pain-in-the-arse parents . . .

—12—

HOW TO BE A PAIN-IN-THE- ARSE PARENT

I must admit at times that I have felt like a pain-in-the-arse parent. You see, I am quite often losing notes and forgetting important dates, so on occasion I have had to shoot off an email like: *Hi, it's Jack's mum here. What time is his assembly on today?*

And with that little query, I become a pain in the arse, for the recipient of my email then has to go and find out when the assembly is, and respond to me.

At other times, I've had to go into the school because ethics classes are about to start and if I don't get the form in yesterday, the kids will be stuck doing the dreary 'Non Scripture'.

'I'm so sorry,' I say. 'I'm not usually one of *those* parents . . .', when in fact that's exactly what I am at that moment.

Pain-in-the-arse parents are a real thing and every school has them. You can see how teachers try to avoid making eye contact with them as they move about the playground, trying to find someone to complain to about something completely ridiculous. So, let's take a look at some behaviours that will definitely make you the topic of conversation in the staffroom.

COMPETITIVE PARENTS

These are the parents who see their kids' achievements as an extension of their own—and they're not satisfied with second place. The crown for Most Competitive Parent undoubtedly goes to the wicked Wanda Holloway. In 1991 Wanda was so upset that her daughter Shanna was not selected for the cheerleading squad at her Texas high school that she arranged for a hitman to kill the mother of one of the girls who did make the team. Unfortunately for Wanda (and fortunately for her intended target), her plans were foiled by her ex-husband, who totally dobbed her in. Wanda served ten years.

Of course, that's an extreme example. There are many less high-profile instances of parents who push their kids to the limits. I'm sure you encountered the mums who brag about how busy they are taking their kids to music lessons and tutoring and sporting activities and language classes so that they 'get ahead'. (This over-programming can actually lead to increased anxiety in children, so my tip is 'less is more' when it comes to extracurricular activities.)

Perhaps you've been caught at the side of the footy field or the swimming pool by some bore who insists on regaling you with details of the amazing achievements of her wonderful daughter.

Then there's your brother-in-law, who wants you to watch the entire soccer match his son played in last weekend, which he taped—ON HIS PHONE.

Like all tedious people, the best way to deal with competitive parents is to look them in the eye and say, 'Sorry, I have to go to the car and get something.' And then go to your car, slip the keys in the ignition, and drive far, far away.

THE TYPE A PARENT

Here come the power parents, the ambitious, business-minded, multitasking go-getters who live to stick to a good rule. Often employed by large law firms or financial institutions, these parents quite often take on the position of the president of the school's P&C. They are generally feared and loathed by the principal, who has to put up with their constant emails and general arrogance. Teachers dealing with Type A parents need to be on the top of their game, as they are a demanding bunch. Homework has to be distributed on the right day, or the world will end. Type A parents are the ones who will enter the classroom when you are in the middle of a mental computation workshop, and think it is perfectly reasonable to demand that you stop what you are doing and enter into a long in-depth discussion about their son's literacy issues.

'Why don't you make an appointment to see me after school?' the teacher might suggest. The Type A parent will pause briefly then recommence her questioning, all the while keeping one eye on the stock market movements on her phone.

Hey, their time is more important than yours. Sit up, take note and thank the lord that you don't have a classroom full of them.

THE SEPARATED PARENT

Children from what used to be called 'broken homes' are just like everyone else in the class—but the same cannot always be said for their parents, particularly those who are recently separated. Separated parents become pains in the arse when they bring that tension into the classroom.

Fights and nit-picking should be left at the school gate. Bringing your super-hot new girlfriend to your kids' kindergarten Christmas concert to parade in front of your ex-wife is not cool. Have a plan; let the teacher know of the joint custody arrangements, if there are any. And focus on your kids' happiness.

THE ENTITLED PARENT

Have you ever pulled up at the lights and seen one those cars that has a sticker on the rear windscreen to let you know which school the driver's kids attend? You know the ones. They're usually on the back of a Volvo four-wheel drive, or maybe an Audi. Well, these parents spend tens of thousands of dollars a year to earn the right to drive around with that sticker.

These are the parents who expect the best of everything for their kids. And fair enough; we all do. But while most of us will send our kids to the local school and play the hand we are dealt, the Entitled Parent has paid exorbitant fees and therefore has huge expectations with regards to the return on their investment. So they will happily turn up to the opening of their school's newest polo field and give their approval to the colour palette chosen for the new archery targets.

And when it comes to teaching their offspring, well, you had better be a Rhodes Scholar.

THE ABSENT PARENT

I dealt with a few of these parents during my short career in the classroom, and let me tell you: they are a massive pain in the posterior. A lot of time is spent chasing up notes and sending home reminders that little Johnny's home reader has not been spotted for a whole term and could we please have it back. Or could you at least can send in $8.50 for its replacement?

There might seem to be an overlap between the absent parent and the disorganised parent, but there is a crucial difference: the disorganised parent at least tries to stay on top of things; absent parents just don't give a shit.

THE TOO-AVAILABLE PARENT

At the other end of the spectrum from the absent parent, you have the parent who is always around. They're there for the morning bell as you carry your coffee across the playground to greet your class (this was before the introduction of policies that mean you are now sent to jail for carrying a hot drink near a child). They're there as you walk your class to the classroom, ready to start the day. They're there as hats and bags are put away. They're there as the students file into the classroom and there as you take the roll. And, as sure as shit, as the afternoon bell blares out, there is that face again, peering through the window of the classroom, just checking out what is going on. The too-available parent is always the first to volunteer to come on the excursions, to do reading groups every day and to spend hours covering books in contact paper.

Still, as I always say, we need all types of people to piss us off. And if you belong to one of the categories listed above, please adjust your behaviour—or rest assured that weary educators are discussing you in most unflattering terms in the staffroom at lunchtime.

—13—

FORGOTTEN VALLEY

I was a fresh-faced twenty-two-year-old when I turned up to school for my first day of being a proper teacher. In retrospect, I realise that twenty-two is far too young to be given the responsibility of shaping and moulding young minds. I was far too green to be thrown in the deep end.

But into the deep end I went.

In 1995 I was assigned my first teaching job, a one-year contract at Macdonald Valley Public School, a small school near St Albans, just outside Sydney. And when I say small, I am not kidding; the staff consisted of the principal . . . and me.

My charges were the infants department; yes I had a whole department of my own! My classroom was an old cottage and I had eleven students from kindergarten to Year 2.

My boss, Mrs Chapman, was a firecracker of a lady; very open-minded and a bit of a hippy—which was probably quite a good fit for the area, as St Albans had its fair share of hippies.

On the first day, she gave me a quick rundown on the local families and characters; to say this tight-knit community of a hundred or so people was diverse was a complete understatement. We had artists and hippies, actors and musicians, fundamental Christians and Ashram members. And given that the school only had twenty-seven students in total, it was not long before I knew them all. And they knew all about me.

The village of St Albans was settled in 1842 and was an attractive spot for farmers to establish crops due to the proximity to the river, which made transport easier. But as railways were extended further west, it earned the nickname the 'Forgotten Valley'. There was a pub, a courthouse and a police station; although in my time only the pub was still used for the role for which it was intended.

At the end of my first day of teaching, I was confronted by a redneck father who looked a lot like Santa Claus (though his beard was much more impressive that Santa's, and contained tobacco and food besides). He demanded to know my qualifications, which I listed, and then my experience, which I also listed: I had one day's experience—and today was the day! Knowing what I know now, I would have told him to jam it up his clacker, but I was twenty-two, remember, and fresh off the boat.

Well, didn't I cop an earful!

I fled to the principal, and I suppose I dobbed. Yes, I dobbed in a parent to the principal. This was going to make me hugely popular in the district.

Mrs Chapman marched outside and gave the man a large verbal serve. You did not fuck with Mrs Chapman. She had no time for crap.

It turned out that my tormentor—the first parent I got to know—was the local mechanic.

I also got to know the school secretary. She was a lesbian who, it transpired, was having a raging affair with one of the school mums.

The school may have been small, but I was learning some huge life lessons very quickly.

✳

I took up residence in the (deconsecrated) church house at Wisemans Ferry, which was said to be haunted by the ghosts of those buried in the graves that were dotted around it. In summer it was as hot as an oven, and in the winter the cold was almost unbearable. (I used to stay one night a week in my classroom, however. Not for any great educational reason, but because I was twenty-two and obsessed with *Melrose Place* and I couldn't get reception at the church house.)

After school on Friday I would walk down to the post office and get a money order made out to the church for the sum of $90, which was the weekly rent. I would usually see two little girls from my class sitting outside the pub opposite the post office, eating a bag of chips and drinking Coke.

'Hi, Miss Murphy!' they would scream, waving madly.

These two friends were in Year 1, with eyes that had seen way more than the average six-year-old. Both were street smart and cunning; they had to be. Their mums were almost always at the pub, and in an inebriated state pretty much all of the time.

The two girls were as different as night and day. One was pale and blonde while the other had the most glorious dark skin and hair. They never got to school on time, but wandered in casually, usually about ten-ish. I had a word to Mrs Chapman, who gave the mothers a lecture on the importance of getting their kids to school on time. Punctuality did improve slightly, but I still kept a close eye on those angels. I gave them breakfast every morning when they arrived and made sure they each had a birthday cake on their special day. When you are a teacher, it is one of the most heartbreaking things to see the kids who are parenting themselves.

My kindy kids were beyond divine. There were only two of them, but they were just so dear. The boy, Harry, was the son of a very well-known Australian actress and Dominique was a tall redheaded girl who wouldn't say boo to a goose. She was a dreamer, while Harry was a showman who was able to throw the most magnificent tantrums I have ever seen.

I warmed to him immediately. He questioned everything and loved science. When his mum had to travel up to Sydney to tread the boards at the Opera House, little Harry would come and stay with me (which I am sure is totally against some sort of Board of Education policy). I had such fond memories of him that I named my first son Harry.

One day, a new family turned up. The father was tall and skinny, and the mum was very timid. They had a boy and a girl with them, both looking terrified, because up until that day they had been homeschooled by the local cult. Well, to be honest, I'm not sure whether it really was a cult, but everyone else called it a cult and I was ignorant. It was a big fundamentalist Christian church with a compound where families lived permanently. I don't know—is that a cult?

Anyway, the girl ended up in my class, and Mrs Chapman got the boy, who turned out to be as close to a psychopath as one could get without actually committing any murders. No bloody wonder those parents wanted a break!

My favourite time of the day was the morning. I'd drive up the hill to school, park the car then pause to survey the scene. Forgotten Valley was the prettiest country you can imagine. On one side was beautiful, lush farmland; on the other was a wide peaceful river.

Most mornings I had to shoo a few wallabies off the front verandah of my cottage/classroom and I would enter to be greeted with the smell of coffee and cigarettes. The teachers' lounge was located in a garage out the back of my classroom, and Mrs Chapman would be there with an assortment of parents, puffing away and drinking huge vats of plunger coffee.

I would spend the quiet hour before the bell rang organising my day. It was quite a challenge, trying to get everyone through the curriculum effectively, and it would have been impossible to do it on my own, so I had parent helpers. I made full use of the fact that I had access to some of the country's finest talent; I had Harry's mum teach drama, and none other than one of Australia's most pre-eminent composers, Nigel Westlake, supported the music program. (He had two sons enrolled at the school.)

My most reliable helper, though, was a woman called Swami Gurupremenanda, who took reading groups. She was a member of the local ashram and had recently left her husband and found herself. She rid herself of possessions and hair, and started a new life for herself and her three kids, of whom two were at our school. Swathed in orange, with her baby strapped to her back and heavily pregnant, Swami Gurupremenanda was the epitome of calm.

Her young sons both had swami names, and it took me a while to get the spelling right: Shreevidya and Krishnamerti. (But looking at that typed out, I fear I could be wrong.) They were vegetarians, and their diet must have been highly dependent on legumes, as they could produce the most eye-watering farts ever to hit a nostril. They also didn't believe in medicines, so when worms were rife in the classroom, instead of being treated with Combantrin, Shreevidya and Krishnamerti (or is that Shrividya and Krishnamurti?) had to drink excessive amounts of salted water.

One day, Swami Gurupremenanda and the boys didn't turn up to school. The next day, they were back, with a new baby girl strapped to Swami's chest. They'd had a teaching day at home the day before, watching their mum give birth on the rug. Then they just got on with the reading groups, as if nothing out of the ordinary had happened.

The year flew by, and before I knew it, I was up to my armpits in Christmas concert preparations. Now, as any teacher knows, your performance for the entire year is judged solely by this one event. It all boils down to your end-of-year concert. Because I had such a variety of faiths in my class, I decided I was not going to do something Christmassy; it wasn't worth the arguments. So instead my kids did a rendition of my old favourite dance song, 'Walking on Sunshine', while Harry's mum helped me put on a play about education, now-and-then style. It was lame-o but the punters lapped it up.

My last day at school was quite emotional. All the kids and their parents gave me gifts—even my little pub waifs had something for me. One gave me seventy cents and the other a half-empty can of deodorant. I accepted their offerings gratefully.

I hugged Mrs Chapman goodbye for the last time and she handed me my reference:

Ms Murphy has excellent communication skills that have been beneficial to the school, encouraging productive interactions between the staff, students, parents and community members.

I'd loved my year in Forgotten Valley, but now I had bigger fish to fry, having bought a one-way ticket to London. Still, the memories of that first year of teaching will remain with me always. Recently, I checked Facebook to see what the Macdonald kids were up to. One of my kids had sadly passed away in a dreadful accident, which made me tear up a bit, but the others were doing well. It was great to have a sneaky peek at how those little faces grew up.

—14—

TO MISS WITH LOVE

My second year of teaching could not have been more different to my first. Fresh from the bucolic peace of Macdonald Valley Public School, I was now standing outside a building that could easily pass for a prison. I had accepted a teaching assignment at Southwold Primary School, in the London Borough of Hackney.

This particular school was as rough as guts, and I had been put in charge of thirty-three eight-year-olds. Despite the obvious challenges, though, I was as keen as mustard, my head filled with visions of Sidney Poitier in *To Sir with Love*. I was going to be the change that these kids were yearning for, the inspiration, the guiding light that would instil in them a lifelong love of learning. I was going to be that teacher they would remember for the rest of their lives. The one who would be mentioned in speeches in years to come, when my charges had gone on to achieve great things.

The school was a few blocks from the bus stop, and I'd had to step carefully around syringes as I walked the cold, dreary route past off-licences and betting shops. The school itself was protected by high security gates. Three storeys tall, it was an imposing sight, with nary a trace of greenery to soften its forbidding exterior.

Taking a deep breath, I entered the gates and made my way to the office, where I announced that I was Miss Murphy, reporting for duty.

The lady behind the desk barely looked up from her paperwork, but just handed me a clipboard and asked me to fill out a form.

'Take a seat,' she said when I handed it back to her a short time later. 'Patricia will be with you shortly.'

The school began to come to life, with small kids streaming through the doors. I was joined in the reception area by a large African woman, who told me that she had to inform the principal about a domestic dispute she was having with her partner, who was not to set foot inside the school ever again.

'What the fuck have I got myself into?' I was asking myself, when a kid burst into the office with what looked like a badly broken nose. He couldn't have been more than seven years old, and he explained to the school receptionist that he had been smashed in the face by someone called Friendly. It turned out that Friendly was a girl in my class, and she had some anger management issues, but more on that later.

The principal of the school was a woman of immense dignity. She walked down the corridor with an air that was positively regal. Stopping first to talk to my friend with the domestic issues, she said something along the lines of, 'Not today, Evelyn. I just cannot deal with this today,' before sending her on her way. She then turned to me.

Standing up, I said, 'Hi, I'm Kayte Murphy—the agency sent me.'

She looked me up and down, then motioned to me to join her in her office. There, having introduced herself as Patricia Downey, she went on to explain some things about Southwold Primary School. Apparently, the school had an Ofsted inspection scheduled for the following term, and the class I had been assigned was adorable and delightful.

Actually, she said the exact opposite.

Of course, the term 'Oftsed' meant nothing to me, and I suppose it means nothing to you either, so let me explain: Ofsted was in fact the Office for Standards in Education, Children's Services and Skills. It was responsible for undertaking a thorough inspection of schools and childcare centres to ensure they were meeting the highest possible educational and administrative standards. Established in 1992 by Prime Minister John Major, the prospect of an inspection had struck the fear of God into the hearts of teaching staff the country over.

By this stage the school bell had gone, so Patricia rose. 'Let's go meet your class,' she said.

I am not going to lie to you; I was shit-scared.

The corridors were deserted as I meekly followed Patricia. We passed classroom after classroom and all were quiet—except for one: the classroom we were heading towards.

Patricia flung the door open and burst through like a cabaret star, bringing instant quiet to the room. There were children everywhere. Unsupervised, they were running riot. It took all my willpower not to turn and flee.

'Class, this is Miss Murphy,' Patricia said, before promptly walking out again.

In the silence that followed the principal's announcement, I heard her footsteps click-clacking back down the corridor.

Sixty-six eyes were locked on my face. I greeted the class, then invited a few of the boys to extricate themselves from each other and take a seat on the floor.

I sat on a chair, but before I could explain who I was and what I was doing there, I noticed one scrawny kid had his hand in the air.

'Yes?' I said, thinking he might have some valuable information to impart, such as how long we had to go before recess.

'I'm really f'rsy, can I 'ave some wa-ahr?'

To which I answered, 'Pardon me?'

'I'm really f'rsy, can I 'ave some wa-ahr?'

I had no idea what he was asking. I stared at him blankly.

Exasperated, he said, 'I just wan' a glass ov wa-ahr, okay?'

A little Jamaican girl sitting next to him explained helpfully, 'Miss, him are t'irsty an' want a drink.'

Thanks to my translator everything was suddenly made clear. I granted the boy permission to get a drink of water.

This instantly led to the entire class needing a drink of water. So I lined them up at the door and off we went in search of some water. Needless to say, I had no idea where the drinking fountains were, but I was helped by a few of the kids.

Once at the bubblers, a full-scale water fight broke out. It was winter and it was not warm, but soon the entire class ended up soaked, including me.

My voice rose to a screech as I pleaded for calm.

A kindly teacher who was on a break rescued me. She restored order and got the dripping students into some sort of a line. She introduced herself to me as Gulcan, and to this day I will never forget her kindness. I will also never forget her words of wisdom.

'Don't give them even the tiniest inch,' she advised, 'or a mile they will take.'

Southwold was officially classed as a disadvantaged school, with 42 per cent of the students eligible for the free school dinner program. Since 1944, children of families on low incomes were entitled to a hot school lunch provided by the government. Margaret Thatcher slashed a sword through the program in the 1980s, insisting that it should be put out to local tender, which the schools would pay for, depending on the financial demographic of their area and the demand. This led to a dramatic decrease in the quality of food provided, as caterers tried hard to turn more profit. I was later to discover that this meal was sometimes the only meal my students would eat all day.

To further compound the disadvantage, 75 per cent of Southwold's student body spoke no English at home. And, it turned out, many of them spoke no English at school either. So my class comprised thirty-three hungry students from racially diverse backgrounds, many of whom were not able to understand me. It was like peeling an onion, revealing a new challenge with every layer.

That first day was full of surprises, but none more than a lad called David. All day, I noticed, he lingered near the edge of the carpet, touching and stroking it as if he had never felt anything quite like it before in his life. My translator told me that David was blind.

This was the sort of information that it would have been useful to acquire in a handover meeting with their previous teacher, but it transpired that the class had so far gone through four teachers in the current academic year. Each teacher had left because of the stress.

I was stunned. Again, my head urged me to flee, but my heart was already lost to this rabble. Did Sidney Poitier/Mark Thackeray abandon his class when faced with very similar circumstances?

No, he did not.

✦

That first day was long and I could not *wait* until the home time bell rang out, but I persevered. I was sitting reading with a small group of children (and I say 'reading' but we really should have been reflecting on the alphabet, because that was where we were at) when I noticed that a fight had broken out at the back of the classroom.

As far as I can work out, the fight had something to do with the conquest of the Greek territory of Cyprus by Ottoman Turks back in 1571. You might think that was a bazillion years ago, but clearly it was still a sore point for some in my classroom.

'Turkish dogs!' yelled Nico as he smashed his rival.

Now, I know that you should not get involved in fights, and you absolutely should not put yourself between warring small men/boys, but I did believe that I had some type of duty of care in this instance and it was up to me to put a stop to the dispute.

I approached the boys, urging peace. And that's when it happened.

After all these years, an image of Mehmet has stayed with me. He was as solid as a rock with a very cheeky smile. Later, I would find out that he had the foulest temper I'd ever encountered, with a colourful vocabulary to boot. But there was something about

120

him that I liked immediately. I don't know where he is now, but I suspect he might be languishing in one of Her Majesty's hotels.

Long story short, I copped one in the guts.

Mehmet took a huge swing at Nico, who dodged away just as I stepped forward. As I felt the wind being knocked from my body, the school bell went. Within an instant the room had cleared, leaving me lying on the floor, gasping for breath. I believe that I might have been in shock. I'm not sure how long I lay there, but when Patricia turned up a little while later to see how I'd got on, I told her, 'Piece of cake.'

—15—

THE INSPECTION

As the weeks and months flew by, my time at Southwold Primary School continued to throw challenge after challenge at me. Perhaps the greatest challenge of all was the girl whose parents had named her Friendly.

She was a walking contradiction when it came to her moniker. She barely spoke, but when she did her speech was aggressive and usually littered with profanities. Her mother was basically a larger version of Friendly. I suspect it wasn't a happy home. Nonetheless, I took the girl under my novice wing, and slowly, very slowly, she started to come out of her hard little shell.

And it was little triumphs like these that kept me going. The day that tough, taciturn girl make a friend was the stuff of dreams. Soon, Friendly and Precious were inseparable.

✶

It was not unheard of to turn up at school one day to find that a new student had joined the class. Or that one had left with no warning. The advent of one new family in particular stands out in my memory.

The Joneses had many children, all of whom were exceedingly skinny with sunken eyes and were riddled with head lice. The children were extremely developmentally delayed. It was quite obvious that we were dealing with a family in crisis. The teachers of the Jones children had to work with the local child welfare agency to make sure that they were coming to school on time, that they were eating lunch and that there were no signs of anything sinister.

As time unfolded, the tragedy of their situation became clear. The Jones children were growing up in a house plagued by incest; their father was also their grandfather. I cannot go into the horrors of the visitation reports that we had to read in order to get some idea of their home environment, but suffice to say it was tragic.

I would look at the Jones girl in my class, her eyes dull and old, and I would try with all my might to teach her to read. If she could just read, I reasoned, she would have more opportunities open to her. Together we persevered, using every spare moment available to us, as I knew that she didn't have too much time left with me. By the time the authorities pressed charges against her father and placed all the children into foster care, Irene Jones could read a book. A small book, but a book nonetheless.

Though the grapevine I heard that Irene and her younger sister were adopted together, joining a happy family. I often wonder about them still. I hope that, despite their dreadful beginnings, their lives turned out okay.

David was another one of my concerns. Being legally blind, he could make out light and shade and that was about it. I demanded of Patricia that I get some help with him, as I was still spending most of my time dealing with the hand-to-hand combat that my students thought was part of the curriculum. The inspection was coming up and I really had to sharpen up my classroom management skills. I was aware, however, that every day that slipped away with David sitting there, doing nothing, was making his future prospects worse. Soon a full-time special-needs teacher was assigned to work one-on-one with David. This was an enormous relief because I could concentrate all my efforts on refereeing the rest of the rabble.

Now, this class had never had a plan, had never had a timetable, and the classroom resources we had been supplied were totally inappropriate. Nevertheless, I managed to knock together a program, which looked like a dog's breakfast given the diverse range of abilities I had to cater for. My one rule for myself was that I was never to lose my shit at the kids, because it just didn't work. Instead, I kept my voice low, speaking slowly and deliberately.

We were getting there.

✷

One of the great pleasures of this time in the classroom was the staff I worked alongside. We were as culturally diverse as the kids. Each Friday we would head up to the local caff for lunch. Oh, how I miss that caff! For a couple of quid, you could scoff down the works: bacon, sausages, mushies, baked beans and grilled tomatoes all nestled under something called a 'fried slice', which was just a piece of white bread that they chucked into the deep fryer. Delicious! I washed it all down with a mug of sweet tea, and felt positively English.

And what teacher worth their weight in chalk would not partake of a few unwinding beverages on a Friday at the pub on the way home? This was where the real action happened, as pints of lager were drained and packets of Lay's crisps were demolished.

It was like we were a secret club. Occasionally, one of your charges would come into the pub with their parents and look at you as if you were an escaped zoo animal, because teachers live at school, don't they?

The week of the inspection arrived, and I did what any decent teacher would do. I bought a huge bag of sweets and showed them to the class, explaining that for every day of that week, while we had our special guests, I would give them all lollies if they behaved. Oh, the power of a good boiled lolly.

So popular and effective did my ploy prove, I was kicking myself that I hadn't thought of this earlier.

I spent a lot of time tarting up the classroom, carefully hanging up the kids' art on the walls, which had remained bare for so long. I taught my kids about tissues, and how they were not just for using as spit balls.

But I still didn't know what the fuck I was going to do about Leonard.

Oh, Leonard. Could you be more revolting if you tried? To be fair, he was suffering from some sort of adenoid problem, which resulted in him almost always sporting two long, thin runnels of mucus streaming from his nostrils.

'Leonard!' I would cry. 'Tissues!'

Leonard was unusually tall for his age, perhaps a result of

125

his African heritage, and was particularly fond of spending long periods of doing nothing much but grunting at me.

'Leonard, please take your seat.'

'Nuh.'

'Leonard, I am going to ask you again, please take your seat.'

'Nuh.'

This would go on and on and on until eventually I would wear him down and he would slowly get up and meander menacingly over to his desk. Just when I thought I had won the battle, he would take his arm and swipe another kid's desk clean of books and pencils.

'Please pick those up, Leonard.'

'Nuh.'

And so it continued.

I say again: what the fuck was I going to do with him, and his rivers of snot and his appalling behaviour? Bribes were not going to work with Leonard, and nor were threats, as he just didn't give a shit. I had to try a different approach.

I decided to befriend Leonard, to try to make him understand that if he didn't sharpen up his act then we would all be screwed. I had made such progress with the rest of the bunch; I was blowed if I'd let him ruin it for everyone.

So I kept Leonard very busy that week. He ran all my errands. He was in charge of giving out books, sharpening pencils, taking the vomiting kid to sick bay. Leonard learnt skills in this time that I hope are still with him today, wherever that may be. Leonard cleaned the blackboard, and took the dusters outside at the end of each teaching session to bash them like buggery against the brick wall to remove the excess chalk. (This had the additional benefit of giving him an outlet to release his natural aggression.) Leonard became my main man and I loaded him up with responsibilities. And, heavens be praised, he began to change.

He stopped threatening others with death, which was a delightful turn of events for all concerned. I persuaded him to always keep a tissue in his pocket, and taught him how to successfully deal with the excess snot production he continued to be plagued by. I even managed to convince him to wash his hands.

And then the dreaded day arrived: the Ofsted inspectors came to my classroom.

I was so proud of my class as they sat attentively while I taught at the front of the room. Then, when I asked them to split up into groups, I marvelled at how they all stood and calmly made their way over to their desks. I was floored when Friendly offered one of the inspectors a chair.

FLOORED.

I had done it. I had had my Sidney Poitier moment. From being punched in the guts on that first day, I now had a class of engaged kids who knew that if I turned up each day, then shit would get done.

My last day at Southwold Primary School was 28 October 1996. Patricia handed me a reference and expressed her gratitude. Highlights of the reference include:

> Kayte took on a very unsettled class with a range of challenging needs with very lively dynamics.
>
> She settled and transformed the class by showing them her commitment, utilising a wide range of classroom and interpersonal strategies, and planning and delivering work

PRIMARY SCHOOL CONFIDENTIAL

which was both stimulating and satisfying for the children while meeting their educational needs.

This was quite an interesting way of describing my teaching style, considering that I basically just bribed everyone to behave.

My departure was certainly tinged with sadness. I will never forget the faces of those students, and their stories are entrenched in my memory. Mehmet and Nico, Friendly and her best mate Precious. Darling, dear David and revolting Leonard. They will always have a place in my heart.

—PART THREE—
AT THE SCHOOL GATE

—16—

KISS AND DROP

One by one they come through the school gate, often clutching the hand of a tired and grumpy toddler who had to be woken abruptly from a nap. In small groups they gather, seeking shade from the heat of the day beneath the trees. They are probably tired too.

They are dressed in a variety of ways. Some are in gym clothes and have been in them all day. Some are in business clothes. Most are women, mums, though there is the occasional father, looking refreshed and relaxed for some reason.

Welcome to school pick-up time, where the minutes tick by so slowly, you could swear that time is standing still.

Then the bell rings—and all hell breaks loose.

Drop-offs and pick-ups are the very important bookends to the school day.

Drop-offs start with the forgotten, which can include but is not limited to the following:

Note

Lunch

Library book

Homework

Ball

Shoes

Thing that they borrowed the day before

Glasses

Hearing aids

Hat

To wear a certain colour/cultural costume/crazy thing, because
it is a day on which they are raising money for something

The money that they are meant to donate towards the above
cause

Manners

Asthma puffer

EpiPen

Medication, accompanied by a signed note and instructions

Money for someone's leaving present

Sunscreen

Drink bottle

Whatever the trend is at the time, for without it your child
will become a playground pariah

Depending on the importance of what has been forgotten, you might find yourself hightailing it back home to fetch it. (If, of course, you can find it.) But more likely than not, the forgotten item will remain sitting on the kitchen bench for the rest of the day.

If you are at the beginning of the school year, drop-offs are an interesting time to observe some spectacular tantrums, as four- and five-year-olds cling to their parents' legs, wailing like banshees as their chubby little fingers are prised away by whoever is on hand.

Those kindy kids! To see a teacher attempt to arrange them into two straight lines is like watching someone try to herd drunken puppies.

I recall the day my firstborn started school like it was yesterday.

We entered a huge hall, filled with weeping women.

'Oh God, how embarrassing for them,' I recall thinking, before handing my child over to the teacher and fleeing the room in tears. I don't know what came over me. I blame hormones. (I blame everything on hormones, including my recently grown moustache.)

There are other emotional, hand-wringing scenes that can occur when you are dropping off and picking up your kids from school. One I hate almost more than any other is the up-down-up.

The up-down-up is the look some mums will give you. You know the one: the quick once-over that takes in every detail of your personal appearance. The women who give the up-down-up are the ones who invariably have perfectly groomed hair, nice fingernails, sensible ballet flats on their pretty feet, and nothing but cold, hard judgment in their hearts. They get their notes in on time, their kids are always well presented and they gather smugly in terrifying groups.

They fall silent when you race in at the moment the bell rings, with your hair askew, eyes still crusted in sleep gunk and morning breath rancid. They've been up for hours baking organic cupcakes in their Thermomixes.

Now, it is my opinion that it takes all types of playground parents to make the world go round. But this particular specimen really irks me.

I can recall waiting at the school gate just recently, looking at my unshaven legs and wondering whether I had actually crossed into the ape species, when I noticed one of the Up-Down-Ups walking towards me.

Immediately I felt like I was back in high school, and Alexandra Langham, the meanest of the mean girls, was on her way over to me to let me know in no uncertain terms that I was a dead shit.

But, no, this mum just did the up-down-up before gliding on past. I thought I had got away with it (whatever 'it' was), but then she turned and said in a creepy faux-posh accent, 'So nice to see you, Kayte.'

I mean, she wasn't even looking at me! She was walking away from me! How could it be nice to see me? I wanted to yell out something to that effect, but then I thought again. After all, who am I to judge? Perhaps that is just the way she expresses herself. Perhaps her need to make me feel like a piece of dog excrement on the bottom of her shoe is born of some deep insecurity on her part.

And that's the thing about school gate politics. You never really know what is going on in other people's lives. For all I know, she might have had some terrible news, or been up all night with a vomiting child. She might have just found out that her husband of ten years has been shagging the twenty-four-year-old from work, the one with the long blonde hair and legs that go on forever. Or, of course, she might just be a rude bitch.

★

As your child works his or her way up through the ranks of grades, you are no longer obliged to run the gauntlet of the other mums; you can begin to consider the 'kiss and drop'. The 'kiss and drop'—boy, is that a game-changer. Once you go there, you will never go back.

You begin by crawling the kerb in your car, inch by excruciating inch, until you reach The Zone.

Once in The Zone, you have two minutes to say goodbye to your kids, during which they suddenly remember everything they forgot (see list above). You may alight from the car while in The Zone, but should you move more than two metres from it, or overstay your two minutes—well, you'd better have a well-paying job to cover the resulting fine. Trust me, I'm speaking from experience.

For me, though, drop-offs aren't the problem; it's the school pick-up where everything turns to a complete shit fight.

The most stressful part of my day had become 3.15 pm. This is the time when I go and pick up the boys from school. It is not stressful because the kids are hot and tired and hungry and bitchy (although that does lend a certain charm to proceedings). No, my issue is with the arsehole parking inspectors who patrol the streets during this time.

I pulled up to collect the kids one day, and there were two parking inspectors in attendance. One walked right up and stood next to my car. Her beady eyes narrowed as she pulled out her iPhone and—get this—set the timer. My beady eyes narrowed as I, too, pulled out my iPhone and set the timer for 120 seconds. We waited. A moment passed. A small trickle of children started to appear, none of them mine.

The parking inspector looked down at her phone then back at me.

I wound down the window.

'Excuse me,' I said. 'Are you timing me?'

'You have one and a half minutes left,' she barked.

At that moment, my son Jack came traipsing through the school gate, meandering along with not a care in the world.

'GET IN THE CAR QUICKLY!' I yelled.

He turned a shocked little face to me. Poor bugger. But with barely a minute left on the clock by this time, and knowing Harry's habit of dawdling, I was getting panicky. I addressed the inspector once more.

'Are you telling me that I have to drive off and come back to get my other kid?' I demanded.

'If you're not gone in forty-five seconds, I will have to book you,' she replied officiously.

I have never despised anyone in my life as much as I despised that parking inspector at that moment. I know she was just doing her job, but I think she would be far more suited to a career in correctional services.

I would be completely shit at being a parking inspector. I would be all like, 'Oh, don't worry about it, take your time. I know what kids are like . . .'

I asked the parking inspector if she would mind explaining to my son that I had not abandoned him and would be back shortly to collect him. I asked her to comfort him if he became upset when he came out of the gates and saw me driving off with his brother in the car.

'I won't know which one he is,' she said, watching the timer.

'That's easy,' I snapped. 'HE WILL BE THE HYSTERICAL ONE!'

With fourteen seconds to go, she started to frame her shot. That is what they do now. They take a photo so that, if you should dream of contesting the fine, they just produce the photographic evidence of your wrongdoing and tell you to shut up and cough up.

Feeling mightily pissed off, I turned the key in the ignition.

Just then, Harry came through the gate. Catching sight of me, he smiled and waved.

'RUN, RUN, RUN, RUN!' I screamed out the window.

It was like a scene from a very tense movie. A movie about a desperate mum trying to pick up her kids from school. I would call this movie: *Mum Smack Down*.

Harry started to run.

And then the parking inspector said—she *actually said* to my son: 'Your mum is about to get into trouble.'

'I AM NOT ABOUT TO GET INTO TROUBLE!' I yelled out the window. And as the door shut behind Harry, and with no time left on the clock, I pulled out of the line. As I drove off, I did what any sensible, mature lady would do. I flipped her the one-fingered salute. But I did it so she could not see it. Because she still had the camera at the ready, and I am sure there is a fine for flipping parking inspectors the bird.

Parking inspectors might give me the shits, but at least they don't freak the living hell out of me in the way that lollipop ladies do.

This one time I had walked the kids to school, kissed them each goodbye and then, my mind completely elsewhere, absent-mindedly crossed at the school crossing. I was waving to the car that had stopped for me when, all of a sudden, there was the most alarming screech . . .

I stopped in my tracks in the middle of the crossing, thinking I was about to be hit by an oncoming car—but no. The screech had come from an extraordinarily pissed-off lollipop lady.

Uh-oh. I had done the unthinkable.

I had attempted to cross the road without permission.

I am fully aware that lollipop ladies across the land do so much to keep our children safe. It is an important job; there is no doubt about it, and I'm not questioning that for a moment. And I will admit that the fault was my mine; my mind was in Disneyland, and not on the task at hand, which was to obey her rules.

'Oh my God, I am so sorry,' I stammered.

'No, you're not!' she retorted and threw her stop sign down onto the road.

By this time, a large crowd of obedient parents had gathered by the kerb, all patiently waiting for the lollipop lady to signal to them that it was safe to move across the road. I really wanted to just die, then and there. I didn't know whether I should go back and join the waiting crowd, or continue forward. So I did what any moron would do.

I stood, cemented to the spot, as cars crossed in front of me and behind me. (It was at this point that I had a flashback to that great arcade game of the eighties. You know the one, right? Frogger?) I was hoping like hell that one of those sinkholes I had recently read about in the papers would appear beneath my feet. Not a huge sinkhole—I didn't want to take anyone else with me; perhaps just a two-metre version.

Eventually, my tormentor must have decided that I had suffered enough humiliation, for she marched towards me, blowing her whistle. She fixed me with her steely gaze until, cowed, I was forced to look away. As I feebly navigated through the crowd coming the other way, I caught a few glimpses of sympathy, and I took this as a sign that I wasn't the first to fall foul of the lollipop lady's militant behaviour.

But lollipop ladies aren't the only militants in the school.

Are we ready to discuss the P&C?

17

PARENTS AND CITIZENS, UNITE

One of the many extracurricular roles that parents take on is that of committee member. From the soccer club to the school fete, many of the clubs and institutions through which your child will pass will rely on parent volunteers for both management and fundraising.

I have done my time on several such committees and most have left a bad taste in my mouth.

I once went to a P&C meeting (only one) at which the president stood up on stage brandishing a pile of papers outlining parents' ideas for fundraising. He then 'filed them in the bin'. Literally. There was a bin there and he chucked the papers into it.

Many parents, when asked if they are 'on the P&C', will recoil in horror at the very thought. This is because the P&C is notorious for power plays, politics, bribery and corruption. Sounds like fun, hey?

So at the top of the heap you have the P&C, the powerbrokers. Feeding into this exclusive, elected group are other committees, such as the Canteen Committee, the Parents Auxiliary, the Band Committee, the Uniform Shop Committee, the Health and Welfare Committee, and the committee for parents who just don't give a fuck. These are known as the No-Shows, the ones who can be relied on not to put their hand up for anything. Some may consider these parents to be the smartest of the lot.

But the truth is that schools need volunteers and committees. I mean, how else would you ever find out the gossip? Do a shift at the canteen, and I guarantee you will come away with all kinds of useless tidbits about people whom you don't even know.

But back to the big kahunas on the P&C committee. The peak body of public school parent groups in New South Wales is the P&C Federation, an organisation that was established in 1912—and was dissolved in 2014 ahead of a revamp. It was in such a shambles that the education minister was forced to step in and give everyone a spanking.

Why?

Because they could not keep their shit together. The federation was positively plagued with bullying and infighting. So if this is happening at the highest level, what do you think is happening at the school down the street?

Bullying and infighting!

The fact is, though, schools just could not run without parent volunteers. The problem is that volunteers are getting harder to find. That's because in 57 per cent of Australian families both parents work.

Although she worked part time, my mum also did canteen. I can still remember the excitement of those days when Mum was on canteen. I also recall being very, very popular with my fellow students that day, as they were all hoping I would choose them to be my best friend, thus giving them the golden ticket to canteen freedom at lunch.

Mum would spread lashings of butter onto pink-iced finger buns and dole them out to me and my friends. These days there would be no bright pink finger bun, but something organic, gluten-free and tasteless, so you would not go back to class after recess all hyped up on sugar. Thanks to the P&C, the good stuff, like finger buns, has been banned from our canteens. And don't get me started on monkey bars . . .

Still, I shouldn't cast aspersions. After all, there's no way I'm putting my hand up to be the president of the P&C. And, frankly, I'm not qualified. The ideal P&C president should have a résumé that includes the following:

- Time spent working as a hostage negotiator for the federal police.
- A business degree and, preferably, an MBA.
- Experience in dealing with trolls on Facebook.
- Previous dealings with the United Nations.
- Some sort of qualification in health and nutrition.
- At LEAST a brown belt in karate.
- Membership of any of the major political parties.
- Superior finger-pointing skills.
- The ability to lip-read.
- The ability to say SOD OFF in several different languages, bearing in mind that we are a multicultural society.

REAL HOUSEWIVES (AND HUSBANDS) OF THE P&C*

Now of course I am generalising here. I am sure most parents and citizens groups are run with no fuss, by intelligent people with no hidden agendas . . . *shifts eyes quickly* . . . but I asked parents from across the country to share with me some stories of what is going on in their neck of the woods, and here are a few gems that came in:

The principal and the president hate each other and once they had to be physically separated at a meeting.

The P&C at our school has been taken over by want-to-be marketing-degree mums who think they know everything!

At my niece's primary school, some of the P&C people started up a little swingers group.

There are a lot of stereotypes about those who get involved. Not all are bad—there are always the quiet, industrious few who just get on with it and don't seek the limelight. Then you have the slightly more ambitious parents (lawyers, teachers, medical professionals in their other lives) who join the executive so they can have a bit more say on how things are done. The treasurer is usually a mum with an accounting or bookkeeping background and multiple children. The secretary—someone with an admin background or (in our case) a work-from-home dad with excellent IT skills and a sharp sense of humour. Then you have the vice-presidents, who are usually best mates with the narcissistic president; often the role of the VP is simply to massage the president's ego. And of course you have the martyr who runs around DOING EVERYTHING, always looking flustered and stressed, but won't say no to the next Bunnings' barbeque or cake stall. You can never thank this person enough.

My P&C time was like being in a Real Housewives of . . . episode. As president, I basically sat there watching insane women go at each other hammer and tongs. You can't help but get caught in the crossfire. I am now studying psychology so I can counsel all their kids when they end up in therapy.

A few years back, a P&C I was involved with had every single committee member resign. There was an epic all-in text/email/phone brawl between the tuckshop supervisor and P&C committee. The tuckshop supervisor believed the food should be both cheap and nutritious, but the P&C wanted the tuckshop to make a significant profit. There was name-calling, food was thrown and many tears were shed.

My favourite story is when someone proposed adding an optional tunic for girls to our uniforms and at the P&C meeting to discuss this a parent stood up and quoted High Court verdicts on human rights. Others brought up the feminist movement of the 1970s. It was the most absurd evening of my life.

*Please note that, the above anecdotes notwith-standing, the author acknowledges that many P&C committees do amazing work, and work in harmony, promoting parental involvement in schools in a rewarding and positive way, without political agendas or power struggles. She just could not find any of them to interview.

18

WHAT'S ON YOUR SANDWICH?

So, let's discuss about school lunches . . . Talk about complicated!
You practically need a degree in nutrition to plan a school lunch
these days. But when did the obsession with the healthy school
lunch begin?

At the turn of the nineteenth century, when compulsory school
attendance was introduced, you were sent to school with a belly
full of porridge. Once there, you would spend the day reciting
poetry by rote and learning other useful life skills. For lunch you
would have bread and jam, or bread and dripping.

Just as an aside, have you ever wondered what dripping is?
I have, so I did a little research . . . When a joint of meat is roasted,
all the fat and sinew drip out and congeal. This 'meat' jelly is
what's known as dripping. It was smeared onto bread, which
was then wrapped up in wax paper and carried to school, often

entombed in a metal tin. By lunchtime, the sandwich had often really heated up and was turned into mush. Nom.

Then in 1922 something happened that would revolutionise school lunches. An outfit called the Fred Walker Company used brewers' yeast to develop a product that they called Pure Vegetable Extract. Catchy, huh? Fortunately, some bright spark changed the name to Vegemite, and out to market it went. And the rest is history, right?

Well, no—not quite. Australians weren't buying it, figuratively or literally; they were already heavily into the English version, Marmite. So in 1928 the Fred Walker Company tried a rebrand; Vegemite was reintroduced to consumers under the name Parwill. Because if Marmite, then Parwill. Get it? And, no, I am not making this up.

As a marketing initiative, it was an epic fail. The name was changed back to Vegemite and, next thing you know, the British Medical Association was getting all excited about its medicinal benefits. It was so jam-packed with vitamin B that they recommended embracing it with gusto.

And with gusto it was duly embraced! Because we love our Vegemite, we all adore our Vegemite; it puts a rose in every cheek. Today we buy over 22 million jars of the stuff, and it is still our most popular sandwich spread.

When I was growing up, sandwiches were still the main staple of the school lunch pail. And by pail, I mean a metal tin. I desperately wanted a *Mork and Mindy* lunch pail. I mean, everyone else had one so why not me? I also wanted a big clunky drink bottle, made of plastic containing plenty of evil PVA to contaminate my Tang. Not that there was any Tang in my pail, for I was a child of the bubbler era, which meant I was either in a serious state of dehydration because the bubblers were broken or I was completely soaked because the bubblers were working a little too well. There seemed to be no middle ground between these two states.

At least we weren't being forced to imbibe warm milk, like those who went before us. From 1950 to 1973, every school kid was given a small glass bottle of milk at morning recess, because it was believed to be beneficial for children's physical health (not to mention the fact that milk makes kids smarter). The problem was that the milk was delivered first thing in the morning, and was generally left out in the sun until recess. By the time it was ready for consumption, it had usually gone off. Many people who went to the school in that era still have an aversion to milk. Thank God for the Whitlam government, who took a look at the scheme and then kicked the bucket over.

Today there are some strong arguments against kids drinking cow's milk, one of the main points being that cow milk is designed to meet the needs of rapidly growing calves, not little children. Some studies have linked cow milk to allergies, diabetes, constipation and ear infections. Anti-cow-milkers might even implore you to replace the milk on your kids' cereal with any of the following:

Soy milk
Almond milk
Rice milk
Goat milk
Sheep milk
Buffalo milk
Oat milk
Hemp milk

Cashew nut milk

Coconut milk

And of course there are fierce arguments ranging around the pros and cons of these too. If you ask me, it can be dangerous to know too much. It can certainly be tedious.

But back to my lunch (the lunch *not* carried in a *Mork and Mindy* pail). Every day I had a Vegemite sandwich on white bread, which may or may not have been fresh, depending on the day. It was inserted into a sandwich bag that had some special kind of closing mechanism that never worked. Next to it was either a banana or an apple. And then there was the treat! The treat was either a Scotch Finger biscuit (with a crunch that was made to share, except I never did) or a bit of homemade slice.

The closest thing I've found to those sandwich bags of yore are Ziploc bags—or, as I like to call them, Mummy's Little Helpers. These little beauties are cruelly shunned by those primary schools with a no-waste policy, but I have spoken to teachers the world over, and here is the hot tip: they love Ziploc bags. They not only use them for their own lunches, they also keep flashcards in them and find them useful for sorting and classifying their colourful plastic counters. But the impact on the environment cannot be ignored, so when you get the letter home from school saying that next Tuesday has been declared a Litter-Free Lunch day, I'd suggest you plan to keep your kids at home. You do not want to fork out for the unbreakable Tupperware litter-free lunchbox again, because it is always used as a soccer ball once its contents have been consumed. And it is not unbreakable. Trust me.

But just what to put in that lunchbox? Government websites have loads of information to guide you through this arduous undertaking. Where once your mum slapped two pieces of bread together and slapped you on the back as you left for school, now you risk social ostracism should another parent spy a pre-packaged item in your kid's bag.

Ideally, your child's lunchbox will contain fruit and vegies, something starchy, something containing protein and something from the dairy family. AND DON'T EVEN THINK ABOUT INCLUDING THAT MINI PACKET OF TINY TEDDIES. I know they are convenient, and I know they will get eaten, but would you let your kid take a loaded gun to school? Some people seem to think that they are essentially the same thing.

I believe the biggest revolution in packed lunches over the years is the box itself. Gone are the days of the tin pail. Lunchboxes these days are insulated satchels complete with a compartment into which you insert a frozen brick to keep the contents cool and fresh. You can even buy lunchboxes that have solar panels, allowing you to heat or cool your food as you require.

My lunches were always hot (though not by design), always Vegemite and always squishy. I recall sitting on the bench one lunchtime—I was in Year 1, I think; at least I was still at that age where the teachers made you sit and eat your lunch before you could go and play. I was always concerned to make sure that my sandwich had the correct margarine-to-Vegemite ratio before I ate it. (I don't know why I was so particular about this.) Anyway, on this occasion, as I opened up the sandwich, I found myself under the flight path of one of those notorious playground pests, the revolting Indian myna bird. This particular myna bird must have been unwell, because it dropped its guts onto my sandwich, adding a spread of its own.

Of course I immediately became completely hysterical and had to be taken to the office for some soothing words and an emergency sandwich.

'A bird pooed on my Vegemite sandwich and I am starving to death!' (I told you I was a drama queen.)

Because it was considered an act of God, rather than the act of a forgetful, hungover or lazy parent who just could not be bothered to pack their child's lunch (like *some* kids' parents ... *ahem*), I was able to go to the canteen and have the kind ladies prepare me a fresh sandwich for free. Needless to say, this fresh sandwich was Vegemite (and I personally supervised the application of margarine and Vegemite to ensure the correct ratio).

All these decades later, I have never forgiven that species of bird for ruining my lunch and scaring the living bejesus out of me. They are still the scourge of Australian playgrounds, and you can find them digging though bins and even in classrooms. Ironically, they were introduced into Australia in the late 1800s to counter a pest problem at Melbourne's market gardens. Who knew they'd turn out to *be* a pest problem? They are one of only three birds worldwide to feature in the top 100 Worst Invasive Species on the Global Invasive Species Database. So, yes, I do bear a grudge ...

Another pest that used to be common in the school playground was the dog. When I was little, there was always a stray dog roaming the grounds, or someone's pet had followed them to school. These dogs were also fond of stealing lunches. (As well as the lunch-stealers, there was this huge labrador who used to swing by from time to time. This beast had a huge set of balls on him, which must have been sending testosterone surges to his brain, as it wasn't lunches he sought out; he was looking for small children to dry hump. The very sight of him coming through the school gate would cause us all to break out into hysterics.)

✳

My journey though the grades coincided with a period of increasing migration. As new families joined our school communities, they brought with them an array of tasty new lunchbox items. All of a sudden I was swapping my Vegemite sandwich for two handmade kibbeh—win! Meanwhile, my Lebanese mate got to acquaint herself with an Australian icon.

A Maori family moved into our suburb and offered to host a Hangi feast at school. This meant that all the male teachers spent the best part of one Friday morning digging a huge hole in the ground next to the cricket nets. A large beast (I'm not quite sure what it actually was, come to think of it) was lowered into the pit and covered with earth. In my memory, there was no concern about occupational health and safety, nor did hygiene seem to be an issue. I do remember that, while I was not a fan of the food (the meat was a bit too fatty for my liking), I loved the spirit of occasion.

Another family who joined us were from Malta. A pair of sour-faced twin girls turned up in our class and I could not *wait* to see what they had in their lunchboxes. Their mum and dad had taken over the milk bar, so when I saw that their lunch pails had exotic-looking little pastries along with full-sized bottles of Coca-Cola, I enquired whether I might partake in a little taste test.

I was refused with a sneer and these stinging words: 'Maybe *your* dad should buy a takeaway then . . .'

Excuse me?!

✷

Speaking of bad playground etiquette, we really should address the issue of scabbing. Heaven forbid you should ever be labelled a scab. That word would follow you around for weeks.

Scabbing, for those not in the know, is the art of persistently nagging your fellow students for either a bit of their ice block, or five cents to buy five carob buds at the canteen. The art to being a good (i.e. effective) scab is to know when to fold, and not simply be a pain in the arse. And of course you had to pay it forward; when approached by someone you scabbed off yesterday with their scabby request today, you had to pay up.

Scab. Such a charming word. You want to know another charming word?

Infestation. But that's a whole other story . . .

CANTEEN DUTY

The secret to a successful canteen duty shift is to listen to the professionals, like the supremely experienced canteen supervisor. Arrive on time, with coffee, and listen while she instructs you. And if you can't be arsed to take on canteen duty yourself, the least you can do is make life easier for those on the front line.

What makes life easier for the canteen ladies? I surveyed some, and here are their responses:

- Do not write orders upside down on the bags. (For some reason, this is a particular irritation.)
- If your ordering bag is chockers with small change, write EXACT MONEY on the bag. It is perfectly normal to go and search around the house for five- and ten-cent pieces. I know this, because I have done it. I have the most success with old handbags and the floor of the car. Even if it is not the EXACT MONEY, write it on the bag anyway. It will save some profanities coming out of your kid's canteen.
- If you write THANK YOU and include a smiley face, your order will be shown to others and you will be declared a lovely human being.

- Please remember to put your kid's name on the lunch order, as well as their class. A plain paper bag with the words SAUSAGE ROLL written on it, and nothing else, is insulting to one's intelligence.

If you really want to win hearts and minds (above and beyond the smiley-face manoeuvre mentioned above), teach your kids the following canteen-lady-approved best practices for making canteen purchases.

- Form an orderly line. Unless you are a new kindy kid—you can do whatever you want, you adorable little munchkin . . .
- Have some sort of idea about what you actually want to order when you reach the head of the line. Don't just stand there like some slack-jawed yokel who had no idea what they were queuing for. And don't then put a fifty-cent piece on the counter, and expect me to read your mind. Unless you are a new kindy kid. You guys can get away with anything, you are so freaking adorable.
- Don't hand me five cents and ask: 'What can I buy with this?' The answer will disappoint you. You cannot even afford the fucking lunch order bag. Tell your oldies to cough up some more cash. Unless, of course, you are a new kindy kid; then you can buy anything you want. In fact, you can have two.

- Use the words please and thank you. If you say to me, 'Can I have a chocolate-chip cookie?' without using the magic word, I will flat out refuse to serve you. Learn some manners! Unless you are a new kindy kid, in which case you can help yourself to the contents of my handbag.
- Don't expect to be able to buy a paddle pop after 1.30 pm. You have no idea why, but there is this big bloody sign stuck up behind the counter. I am sorry, kindy kids; if it were up to me, you would eat nothing other than rainbow paddle pops ALL DAY LONG.
- Understand that those hot cheese rolls do not just appear out of the sky. The mini party pies don't get themselves into the warmer on their own. And the carrot sticks are lovingly prepared by hand; they do not emerge from the ground wrapped in foil and labelled CARROT STICKS. And so I repeat my fourth point: say please and thank you.

All hail to the canteen ladies and men out there. You do good work, sometimes under very difficult conditions. And if you are anything like me, and have mental computation skills that are completely shot to shit, you will know just how physically and mentally draining this canteen business can be.

Speaking of canteens? Where have the finger buns gone? In fact, where did the whole essence of flavour go? The shift towards the 'healthy' canteen began when I was in Year 5, I think, when our canteen swapped chocolate buds for carob buds. For those not in the know, carob is fake chocolate and has a gritty, powdery taste and, in no stretch of anyone's imagination, is it anything remotely like chocolate. It tastes like dirt.

There has been a slow but persistent change in how we feed students via the canteen. We now have someone called 'The Canteen Conveyor', whose prime job is to strip the joint of anything that might be actually enjoyed by the children. I am sure that this person will not be happy until all we can offer the kids are some steamed organic yams and some alkalised water.

And I will not be content until the Sunny Boy is back in a freezer near you. Some traditions should not be tampered with. Now, excuse me while I go julienne these carrots.

19

IT STARTED WITH AN ITCH . . .

Have you ever been on the receiving end of a note like this?

> Dear Parent,
>
> It has come to our attention that several children in your child's class are packing parasites in their hair.
>
> Commence panicking now.
>
> Regards,
>
> Class Teacher (who is now wearing a shower cap)

If so, you are not alone. At any given time, regardless of socioeconomic factors, the scalps of between 20 and 40 per cent of kids in Australia are being feasted on by head lice. (You can stop scratching now; you have probably been spared.)

I have had several experiences of nit-wrangling. It quite often starts when I observe one of the kids mindlessly scratching their hair. Said child is dragged into the kitchen and deposited near some natural light, while I drag a teeny fine-toothed comb through their locks. Most of the time, we are in the clear, but on the odd occasion . . . BINGO.

Nits are nothing new; in fact, they have been around since Jesus was playing halfback for Nazareth. Head lice have even been found on the mummified bodies of ancient Egyptians.

As a wingless insect with useless legs, they are unable to jump, so travel from host to host by direct contact only. They feed on blood and can only live for a short time without a hit of human haemoglobin. It does not matter if you hair is clean or filthy. They do not discriminate or care.

Primary schools are a hotbed of infections. Let's have a look at some of the epidemics you are likely to encounter inside the school gate—starting with my personal favourite . . .

GASTROENTERITIS

Known as gastro, it is my number one 'go-to' excuse when I want to get out of something. Telling someone you have gastro elicits immediate sympathy and your excuse is accepted without hesitation—because no one wants to catch it from you. The thing about gastro is that it is highly contagious. Spreads faster than wildfire.

If your kids are struck down by gastro, here are some handy hints for you, starting with: STOP EVERYTHING! Make sure you are in tiptop condition yourself as you are in for a rough ride. Then get yourself off to the hardware store and purchase:

- The protective clothing that people wear when they are removing asbestos from old houses.

- Two large buckets per child.
- An industrial container of bleach.
- Large sheets of plastic and duct tape.

And on your way home from the hardware store, stop at the chemist for some electrolyte products (for the kids) and then hit the drive-through bottle shop for some medicinal vodka (for you). The above items will not necessarily save you from a spin on the nauseous ride yourself, but at least you'll save the couch.

A GHASTLY TALE OF GASTRO

Of course, you can never really be prepared for gastro. It's just too unpredictable. This is tale from a fellow school mum:

Look, this is something I have never told anyone, mostly because it's just so embarrassing. But what the hell, here goes . . .

A few years ago I was recovering from a very nasty bout of gastro. I had no choice but to do the school pick-up. It had been twenty-four hours since my last brutal visit to the toilet, but I took a bucket with me, just in case a vomit emergency occurred during the thirty-minute round trip.

I pulled up to the pick-up zone at 2.55 pm and waited patiently for the kids to finish school.

My stomach started making all sorts of crazy noises, resulting in the most horrific-smelling fart. Not thirty seconds later, as I was basically being overcome with fart fumes, the teacher on pick-up duty tapped on my window to have a chat.

Without thinking, I wound the window down and BAM! The poor thing was greeted with the most hideous smell I have ever produced.

She sort of took a step back, while I started chatting in a very animated way, waving my arms around in a pathetic attempt to somehow get rid of the smell. Honestly, it was the most awkward three minutes of my life and NEVER have I been happier to see my two kids walk towards the car at 3 pm so I could get the hell out of there!

Trust me, my friend, you would have been discussed in the staff meeting that afternoon.

Kids with gastro are miserable to deal with. Taking a sip of water can trigger a barrage of bodily fluids from every available orifice, and you had just better hope that there is a suitable receptacle nearby.

An early sign that gastro has arrived at your school is a lack of appetite. This will shortly be followed by supreme vomiting and crapping, the likes of which you have never seen before. Your child will complain of severe stabbing pains in the stomach; this is because there is an infection in the guts.

Soldier on, Mama, and cancel whatever you had planned for the next four days.

'SLAPPED CHEEK' DISEASE

I first encountered this little viral infection when I got a call at work. It was the daycare centre, asking me to come and pick up my four-year-old son as he wasn't feeling too great.

The next morning, said son wandered into the room and I got the shock of my life: it looked like someone had given him in almighty slap across the face.

Welcome to 'slapped cheek' disease, a nasty little ailment caused by human parvovirus B19. It's contracted in the same way as most viruses: if an affected kid coughs in your face. The problem is, by the time it can be identified by the sufferer's red cheeks, it's too late; they have already passed the disease around.

There is nothing you can do but treat the resulting flu-like symptoms and wait for the next weirdly named virus to come and say hello.

HAND, FOOT AND MOUTH DISEASE

High temperature? Sore throat? Cranky as fuck? Little blisters on your mouth, your tongue, hands and feet? These are the symptoms that herald hand, foot and mouth disease. Try to steer clear of the blisters, which can burst and secrete a liquid, which is one of the ways it is spread. Lovely! One redeeming feature of the disease is that it only a mild illness and doesn't hang around for long.

CHICKEN POX

My nemesis. One disastrous summer, I was responsible for spreading chicken pox to no fewer than six families. Well, it wasn't me personally, but my virus-ridden offspring. Of course I didn't do it deliberately! I'm not that much of an arsehole.

You see, we were holidaying with several other families, enjoying a glorious summer, with long days on the beach and long evenings of barbeques and beer. The kids all played together nicely; it was positively idyllic.

Little did we know the evil that was about to be unleashed.

A spot. A tiny spot. So small, all alone. Nothing, really.

But within an hour, it had a couple of mates. Uh-oh . . .

By the end of the day, my child looked like an angry red dot-to-dot puzzle.

Within weeks, the epidemic had spread to all the children who had summered together; even those who were immunised were not spared a mild dose. But it was the father of one of the holidaying families who was hit hardest. His face was probably described as an untarred road, and for two weeks he spent his time either in the bath or in bed.

Again, apologies to all those affected. And now, let's now put it behind us.

FEBRILE SEIZURES

There are more childhood diseases than you can poke a stick at. We've got your mumps and your flu. What about measles and whooping cough? And then you have your allergies and asthma. But I ducked and weaved around these common ailments when I was a kid. I went for something much more dramatic, something more attention-seeking, something way more serious . . .

The febrile seizure!

I am not sure how it began, or even why, but sometimes I would heat up like a little radiator and then have a fit. Because I never saw it happen from the outside, I've had to rely on my mum to describe exactly what happened. Apparently it was not relaxing for her.

She has related times when she was driving along and glanced into the rear-view mirror only to see me behaving like I had been placed in an electric chair, with my eyes rolled back in my head. She would pull over and stick her finger in my mouth to hold my tongue down so I didn't swallow it. According to Mum, I damn near bit her finger off!

She took me to specialists all over Sydney, each of whom ran tests on me. Not one of these specialists could give her a diagnosis. So the seizures just became a part of my everyday life.

'Mum, she's having a fit again,' one of my siblings would call out casually, and Mum would race in to find me having a seizure while said sibling calmly continued watching *The Wonderful World of Disney*. I would come to just in time to catch the end of *Herbie Goes Bananas*.

'Mum, she's doing it again . . .' And Mum would race out to the backyard to find me fitting away while we tried to put the cat into a dress.

My febrile seizures were responsible for mum turning prematurely grey, so she says.

It turned out that this was not a serious condition, but it was potentially embarrassing, especially if you accidentally pissed your pants in front of your friends. After a few months of keeping everyone on their toes, the seizures became less and less frequent, until one day they stopped.

I'd lost my party trick.

WORMS

Every few months, Mum would give us a special treat—an unusual kind of chocolate, which had a gritty kind of texture.

Coincidentally, this usually happened at a time when we were horrendously whiny.

'You must have worms!'

Or had insatiable appetites.

'You must have worms!'

Or could not stop scratching our bottoms.

'You must have worms!'

Worms seemed to cop the blame for most things, and it is a tradition that has carried over to the next generation. But what exactly are they?

Threadworms are disgusting parasites that can grow up to 1.5 centimetres long. Apparently you can look for them around the anus, but I'm more inclined just to assume the kids are carrying them if any of the common symptoms occur, and treat accordingly. It is not the actual anus that worries me, but what I would do if I actually spotted a worm. Which I assume would be to hurl my cookies.

You get worms from direct contact with people who have them, or by touching doorknobs, taps and the like that have been touched by people who have them. And much like head lice, they do not discriminate.

✶

The sad fact is, if you have kids at school, you will come across one, two or all of the wonderful extras that goes along with students sitting in close proximity, sneezing and coughing on each other, scratching their bumholes and opening doors. It is just a fact of life.

And unless you build a sheep-dip type contraption at your front door, such ailments are here to stay.

scratches head

20

O CAPTAIN!

O Captain! My Captain! Our fearful trip is done,
The ship has weather'd every rack, the prize we sought is won,
The port is near, the bells I hear, the people all exulting,
While follow eyes the steady keel, the vessel grim and daring;
But O heart! Heart! Heart!
O the bleeding drops of red,
Where on the deck my Captain lies,
Fallen cold and dead.

WALT WHITMAN

Okay, so primary school politics is probably not as dramatic as that, but there is a certain amount of intrigue regarding the selection process of the school leadership team. To be honoured with a school captain's badge—well, that is just about the highest pinnacle of achievement for parents all over the country.

And my parents should know, with a strike rate of four out of five. The fifth being me.

I was the black sheep of the shining, socially brilliant, thoughtful, intelligent and sporty band of siblings that gathered at the family dining table each evening. As the rest of them rattled off lists of the day's achievements, I would push my food around my plate in silence. Occasionally I was able to regale them with irrelevant tales, like how I got assaulted by Libby Taylor.

Hell, even though it's irrelevant, I bet you'd like to hear it too . . .

Each Thursday after school, I caught the bus to the local pool for my swimming lesson. And each Thursday, I would be followed from the bus stop to the pool by the evil Libby Taylor, a girl whose excessive nastiness was matched by her exceedingly good aim. Lizzy would chuck rocks and insults at me for about a block. I found it very traumatic.

But my weekly agony at the hands of Lizzy Taylor evoked no interest, not when my siblings were getting picked for the debating team, winning a scholarship to this or that, or going on some student exchange to Dubbo (where you were to be billeted out with a family that hopefully were quite normal, and not vegetarian!) or, the holy grail, being elected school captain.

The school captain was actually elected by the students, so you'd think that the most popular kid at school would romp it in. But that never happened, because quite often the most popular person was the least suitable person, so in the end the staff chose.

Still, the candidates had to go through the motions, running a campaign in which you shared your vision for the school and implored others to vote for you. There was a speech, a presentation and many meet-and-greets. Ambitious mothers would bake cupcakes all night for their offspring to give out as bribes.

The ideal school captain is an all-rounder, involved in all aspects of school and community life. It helps if you are academic, sporty, do something with a musical instrument and, maybe, just maybe, are slightly religious. The challenge is that you need to appeal to both students *and* teachers. So on the one hand you need to convince the punters that you are very likely to cut the length of the school day dramatically and are committed to having a vending machine in every classroom, while on the other you have to suck up to the teachers. Perhaps remind them that you haven't had a sick day all year, as much due to your commitment to your academic career as to your robust health. And volunteer for everything! Put your hand up to visit old people in the local aged-care home. Bring in a cake for the teachers to enjoy at their staff meeting. Run the MS Read-a-thon, the Skip-a-thon, the Mother's Day stall. Be everything to everyone. But be aware that even this strategy might fail.

The shit really went down at one Catholic primary school in the Hunter district of New South Wales when, despite the student vote overwhelmingly favouring two popular students, the principal relegated them to the lesser positions of vice-captain and instead awarded the top jobs to two kids whose parents worked in the Catholic education system.

There was such an outcry that the local diocese was forced to carry out an investigation into the voting process. The principal was cleared of any wrongdoing. Dirty deeds, done dirt cheap? Perhaps. But let us remember that we are talking about eleven-year-olds here.

Despite my parents' encouragement, I didn't even bother to run for the position of school captain. It was obvious to me that Kim

Johnson had it in the bag. I mean, she was a state runner, for Christ's sake! She was smart, she had hair that always looked shiny and nice, and her uniform was always impeccably ironed. She was not likely to kiss any boys in the library at lunchtime behind the hanging wall of big books, nor was she likely to sit up the back of the bus. Kim Johnson danced in a wholesome way at school socials. While me? Not so much.

The standout of the whole campaign that year, however, was this one boy who gave his nomination speech in the accent of Michael Crawford's character Frank, from the British TV series *Some Mothers Do 'Ave 'Em*. He had the whole school weeping with laughter. From memory, he even kind of looked like Frank.

'Oh, Betty . . .' he would begin, causing us all to erupt hysterically.

On completion of his speech, he waved his hands in victory, and was promptly given a standing ovation.

He did not get the role. But he should have.

My older sister (school captain, North Richmond Public School, 1984) has three children, all of whom were school captains. She is considering running some sort of course in how to groom your kids for greatness.

But, really, does being a primary school captain have any bearing on the future course of your life? Are you likely to get that promotion into middle management because you won a school election twenty years ago?

The short answer is no. No one cares. At the time it can be a huge big deal, but the truth is, it means nothing. Bragging rights for your parents, but that's about it. Oh, and you get to sit on the stage during assemblies.

SCHOOL MOTTOS

Here's another inspiring story about the perils of primary school:

My school motto at primary school was 'Be Sensible'. Forget inspiring Latin quotes, strive and you will achieve, what we receive we shall pass on. We were far more practical at Narrabeen North—'Be Sensible'. I probably should have taken this on board one sunny spring day at little lunch when I decided to do the death drop off the monkey bars. You perched yourself in a sitting pose on top of the bars and then fell backwards with your legs looped around the bar resulting in a perfect dismount, or in my case a broken arm. The ambulance in the playground was exciting for all. The best part of this story is that later that day at lunch time my friend was demonstrating to a large audience how I had broken my arm. Amanda was very good at the death drop but her luck had run out. She also broke her arm, two ambulances in the playground in one day—and Amanda and I became primary school legends.

21

WE ARE GATHERED HERE TODAY

Ah, school assemblies. Has there ever really been a need for them?

Our school assembly was the most bum-numbing, brain-sapping, head-scratching (if you had lice) time of the week. We would file into the old hall, where we were seated according to our year level, with kindy kids up the front and Year 6 down the back. The hall was invariably like an oven in summer and an igloo in winter. These climatic extremes were combated either by two listless ceiling fans or a single lame bar heater.

The hall was a traditional one, with a stage up one end bedecked with nasty old red-velvet curtains with gold trim. On the walls were hung Boards of Merit, listing past school captains, principals and recipients of the dux award. The rest of the decor was given over to fire extinguishers and plentiful signs to indicate the whereabouts of the fire escapes. The hall was adjacent to the canteen, you see, where the cooking was done, and the whole thing was made of timber.

The deputy principal, wearing long shorts, long socks and slip-on shoes in a pale hue, would tell us all to shut the fuck up (but in slightly more acceptable words), and then he would do that trick where you just stand there . . . doing . . . nothing. (Yes, the old waiting trick I went on to use myself when I was a teacher.) He just stood there, hoping that us kids would eventually notice that he was about to completely lose his shit and quieten down. Sometimes it worked, but more often it didn't, so he would make an example of someone, usually Shane Ryan, and send him or her to the office with the promise of dire consequences for his rowdy behaviour. This was usually enough to induce the rest of us to, well, shut the fuck up.

'Please stand.'

The deputy would then invite Year 3 teacher, Mrs Browne, who was eighty-seven in the shade, to lead the school in singing 'God Save the Queen'. Watched on by a portrait of the great lady, we would tunelessly bellow our expressions of loyalty.

'Please be seated.'

We sank back onto the floor (those cold hard floorboards were a pain in the arse, literally) as, one by one, self-important teachers stood up to hector us on dull subjects like rubbish bins, or bike racks, or one of any number of other things that we were doing wrong.

It was then time for the Assembly Item. Perhaps, for something different, the Year 1 class might favour us with a percussion version of 'Popcorn.'

And then we were on to the class awards. This was when the principal himself, a man in long shorts, long socks and slip-on shoes in a pale hue, would make an appearance. Scratching his moustache, he would ask us to please wait until the end of the ceremony to show our admiration for the chosen ones.

'Class KM, Jenny Bolton, for having a wonderful smile . . .'

And the crowd would go WILD!

The principal would remind us to please save our applause until the end.

'Class 1S, Brett Dalrymple, for going a week without crying . . .'

Hysterical cheering, thunderous applause.

Sighing, the principal gave up, and rattled through the rest of the list as quickly as he could.

When at last he was done, he would ask us to stand for the school prayer.

This is our school
Let peace dwell here
Let the room be full of contentment
Let love abide here
Love of one another
Love of life itself
And love of God.
Let us remember
That as many hands
Built a house
So many hearts
Make a school.
Amen.

And we would singsong away, without a clue as to what it actually meant.

22

LET US PRAY (OR NOT)

Whether you were religious or not, scripture classes were an inevitable part of primary school when I was growing up. Sure, there were the odd outliers, like the kids from the Jehovah's Witness family who got to go outside when we recited the school prayer in assembly. These same kids would also avoid any religious-based festivities. I remember being aghast to learn that they didn't get birthday gifts or Christmas presents. I mean, where was their incentive to keep living?

For the rest of us, though, scripture classes were just another part of the curriculum, like art or sport. Your parents had the choice to send you to either Catholic or Church of England, and that was it. The Jehovah's Witness kids went to the library. Welcome to your first experience of segregation based on religion!

The scripture teachers were all elderly members of the local churches, and try as they might, they were unable to maintain control over any of the classes I attended.

It is safe to say we Woogs are not religious. (Although I probably should be thankful I am here at all. You see my dad was training to be a priest when my mum stole him from Jesus. Boom, chickie-bow-wow indeed.)

When it was time for my eldest to start primary school, we had to decide which scripture he should do. Mr Woog has an extreme aversion to organised religion and was insistent that he did 'non-scripture', whereas I was of the opinion that if there were lessons in anything on offer, then we should put our hands up.

So we decided that our kids would study a year of every faith, starting with Judaism. My kids are across that now, as well as Baha'i, Catholicism and Church of England (well, their basic principles at the very least).

Me? I worship weekly at the Church of Chatswood Chase, our local shopping centre, where the congregation are expected to wear tight jeans, long black boots, a white long-sleeved t-shirt under a puffer vest, and finish it off with a Bugaboo Pram. There may also be a Pandora bracelet involved.

Our local public school has been trialling ethics classes in the upper years, which I think is terrific. The aims of the ethics classes are as follows:

- To introduce the language of ethics and, in doing so, to provide the tools to survey the values and principles we live by.
- To encourage openness towards important personal and public issues.

- To introduce dialogue as a means of resolving ethical issues.
- In short, to deepen the ethical sense of future generations.

These ethics lessons are designed to teach you to be a more thoughtful person. And, in my opinion, everyone could do with a dose of that.

But then enter a dinosaur: a fella by the name of Fred Nile.

Fred Nile is (or was, depending when you are reading my book) the leader of the Christian Democratic Party, a political group that promotes Christian values in Parliament and evaluates all legislation on Biblical principles.

He also HATES the thought that our kids can learn ethics at school. HATES.

The truth is that ethics has nothing to do with religion, but Fred insists that it will affect the 'bums on seats' movement. Ethics is a strand of philosophy, and heaven forbid our kids might make meaningful and empathetic decisions on their own.

Considering a lot of our politicians are morally bankrupt themselves, is it any wonder that this is not a mandatory part of the Australian curriculum?

23

CRIME AND PUNISHMENT

At my primary school, the most feared punishment was detention—though detention's bark was worse than its bite. There were a lot of myths circulating about what happened when you were on detention. One was that a teacher would draw a dot of chalk on the blackboard and you had to spend the entire lunchtime standing with your nose pressed to that dot. Another was that you would be forced to stand against a wall in the blazing sun for an hour with your hands on your head as your peers played in front of you.

The reality was not as physically arduous, although it was indeed degrading: you had to spend the lunch hour in a supervised classroom writing out your crime with the words 'I must not' in front of it.

I must not throw a duster at Morris's head
I must not throw a duster at Morris's head

I must not throw a duster at Morris's head

I must not throw a duster at Morris's head

I must not throw a duster at Morris's head

I must not throw a duster at Morris's head

I must not throw a duster at Morris's head

I must not throw a duster at Morris's head

At the end of lunch, you took your lines up to the teacher/ warden at the front and showed her.

She would ask the question: 'What must you not do?'

'I must not throw a duster at Morris's head.'

And back to class you would go, to look at the back of Morris's head, which still had a faint chalk mark on the back of it. And it was all you could do not to empty the contents of your sharpener down the back of his shirt . . . Or so I am told.

Back in my day, a bit of physical and emotional abuse was an accepted part of the school day.

Take my Year 5 teacher, Mr Golloway. A tall, thin man whose face was stamped with a permanent sneer, you could describe him as 'old school', which is another way of saying he hated children.

Mr Golloway's favourite pastime was humiliating his students. He would quite often throw a chalk-laden duster at me with alarmingly good aim, and yell: 'Sit down, you drongo!'

The reason I was standing in the first place was because each morning we had to recite our times tables. I was completely stuck on the sevens. Mr Golloway would draw a circle on the backboard and write the numbers 1 to 12 around it. First he would choose a number, and then he would choose his victim.

If your name was called you would stand and wait while Mr Golloway readied his stopwatch. His eyes would narrow, his lizard-like tongue would dart out to wet his thin mean lips, and then he would yell: 'GO!'

And if it was me who was standing, I would simultaneously freeze and wet my pants a little. Then, panicking, I would stammer and stutter out random numbers, hoping that some of them might even be right. Eventually Mr Golloway would crack the shits and peg the duster at me.

'Sit down, you drongo!'

Although sometimes he would mix it up a bit and call me a dunderhead. Just for shits and giggles. When he got completely fed up, he would order us all to do silent reading, while he went out to the car park to have a smoke.

Now imagine the repercussions today if a primary school teacher, or any teacher for that matter, threw an object at a student (other than a ball during PE) and belittled said student with unflattering names? There would be an international outcry.

As recently as 2014, it was suggested that Australian students might actually benefit if we were to bring back corporal punishment. A so-called expert by the name of Kevin Donnelly actually argued that bringing back the cane would stem the rising tide of suspensions that are handed out each year.

Corporal punishment was phased out in the late 1980s, but I still have vivid memories of kids copping the cane at school. You would see them coming out of the principal's office, massive welts on the palms of their hands. It was enough to scare me straight.

On the upside, corporal punishment was swift at least. Many schools now have discipline policies that would rival *War and Peace* when it comes to complexity and length. Here's a typical step-by-step outline of the punishment process:

- Offending student reminded of what constitutes acceptable behaviour.
- Student given time out.
- Student moved to another class.
- Student moved to an isolated room.
- Behaviour plan negotiated.
- Parents invited into the process.
- Interagency referral team contacted.
- Student suspended.
- Re-entry plan negotiated.
- Parents reflect on when it all turned to shit.

When you think about all those hours, all those resources and the cost incurred following the procedures outlined above, a couple of sharp ones can start to seem like a better way to go. But then you consider the effect on a child of the physical abuse and emotional turmoil. Mr Golloway's approach was hardly beneficial to students; just ask Shane . . .

Shane started at our school in Year 5 and, like me, he was in Mr Golloway's class. Shane was tall and handsome, with hair as black as night, and even at the age of eleven you could see he was headed for trouble. Which, of course, was extremely appealing.

Yes, I fell for the boy from the wrong side of the tracks. And I mean that stuff about the wrong side of the tracks literally; I lived in Windsor and he lived in South Windsor, on the other side of the rail line that divided the haves from the have-nots. South Windsor was known for its transient population and public housing tenants. It was rumoured that Shane's dad was incarcerated in the local prison, that he'd been convicted of armed robbery. (Although I must stress, this was just a rumour; there was no evidence to back it up.) My infatuation with Shane was unrequited, however; as far as he was concerned, I was just some dork who didn't know her times tables.

Right from the outset, Mr Golloway and Shane were engaged in a mighty battle of wills. From the moment they first locked eyes, it was game on.

Mr Golloway would order Shane to stand and undergo the dreaded times table challenge, only to be met with a firm 'nup'. If the teacher insisted, Shane would quite openly flip him the one-fingered salute, which would drive Mr Golloway incandescent with fury.

Shane had the attitude and swagger of a fifteen-year-old. A really fucked-up fifteen-year-old who was on a one-way ticket to juvie. He spent an inordinate amount of time sitting outside the principal's office, under the watchful eye of the office ladies.

And then one morning he did something totally bizarre.

He rode a horse to school.

He cantered into the playground on a huge pinto horse, and we all went hysterical—some with glee, others with fright.

The word soon reached the staffroom, where a meeting was taking place. Mr Golloway rushed to the scene, his face purple with rage as he demanded that Shane bring the horse to a halt.

But Shane ignored him. Around and around the playground he went, faster and faster on that huge horse, heedless of the kindergarten kids or anyone else who got in his way. Finally, after one last lap of the playground, he stuck his finger up at the lot of us and shot out of the front gate, never to be seen again.

FEAR OF EMBARRASSMENT

We all fear humiliation in the playground. This story is mortifying:

> For me primary school was all about the morbid fear of being embarrassed. By parents; by younger siblings; by teachers. This is probably as a direct consequence of the excruciating moment for all of us in 5L when, on a camping excursion to the Warrumbungles, one of our class sat on a bull ants' nest. In response to the girl's screams, Mrs Gore lifted the girl up off the nest and without any consideration of the true consequence of her actions, pulled down the girl's undies. In front of us all. It was like a car crash—you just couldn't look away.

24

LIFE IS A CELEBRATION!

If there is one thing that primary schools across our fair nation like to do, they LOVE to celebrate! Heck, they even teach Celebrating Together as a unit in the Human Society and Its Environment curriculum. (This is what we used to call Social Science if you can remember that far back.)

I have a friend, who you will meet in an upcoming chapter, who is a Gets-Shit-Done Mum. She texts me whenever there is a celebration on.

BEEP BEEP—Harmony day. Wear orange.

You want to know something? My kids both have a severe lack of orange clothing, so they tend to wear red and white and ask their teachers to look at them through blurry vision.

BEEP BEEP—NAIDOC week. Kids need $2 each for damper making.

I could think of nothing more disgusting than eating burnt on the outside, raw on the inside globs of dough that have been pummelled by hundreds of grotty hands. No. Thank. You.

BEEP BEEP—Crazy hair day. I have checked with the chemist and they have run out of coloured hairspray. Just thought I would let you know.

Of course the chemist has run out of coloured hairspray because they are a chemist, not a bloody two-dollar shop. Crazy hair day has caught me out for an impressive six years now. I get creative with gel.

BEEP BEEP—Year 6 cupcake stall today. Send cupcakes. Label your container so you can get it back.

I choose to totally ignore this text.

BEEP BEEP—Don't forget that it is the sports carnival today!

Much like a ballet concert, you wait around for hours and hours to spend a few seconds watching your kid run in a race. You get sunburnt as buggery, go slightly deaf from all of the war-cries and talk to the other mums about how darn hot it is. The sports carnival is also a place where swarms of flies like to frequent.

BEEP BEEP—You are on canteen duty RIGHT NOW. RUN!

This is a common occurrence because of my lack of respect for communications.

My friend is such a useful person in my life. I should really put her on the payroll. You see, our school newsletter is now delivered via an app, and I tend to ignore it. I know, we are all trying to be environmentally friendly these days, but paper works best for me.

BEEP BEEP—It is book week.

Book week should be re-named piss-weak when it came to my own efforts as a kid. I was an avid reader and I was deeply invested in *The Folk of the Faraway Tree*. Jo, Bessie and Fanny were totes cool in my opinion, and I even began to warm to Connie. But I had a non-sewing mum and one year things were very desperate, so I just grabbed the sheet from my bed and went as a ghost.

When I had to tell my character's name to the teacher who was announcing to the crowd what the kids were actually dressed as, I had no idea. So when it was my turn to walk around the quadrangle, she announced verbatim what I had said: 'And here is a ghost from some book of her sister's whose name she has forgotten . . .'

I mean, how many ghosts could I have come up with on the spot? Surely Casper. But I was known as the 'ghost from some book of her sister's whose name she has forgotten' because my imagination was having a wee holiday.

THE SWIMMING CARNIVAL

The swimming carnival is the great leveller of playground politics.

I recall a near-drowning experience of my own when trying to complete the 50 metres as a wee tacker. Fuck winning the race; it was a matter of survival and trying to avoid the ultimate public humiliation of being fished out by a giant pole.

I do remember, however, the highlight of the swimming carnival was the canteen at the pool, which stocked, among other things, Redskins and Wizz Fizz. This is where you most likely would have found me.

These days, like most things, we have got far too structured and there is scheduled FREE PLAY at the modern swimming carnival, although there is quite often a very lolly-centric canteen much to the delight of the students.

Woogs are not known for great swimming abilities, and I am grateful for this. Those gifted with supreme swimming abilities have very sleepy parents who drive them to early morning training. And that gig is something I can avoid, THANK GOD.

One thing I have noticed is that kids who are gifted with great swimming abilities more often than not have multiple siblings who are also similarly gifted. In my day, it was the Upton sisters who dominated the pool. There were three of them—Susie,

Julie and Kathy—and they could all be relied on to (pardon the pun) sweep the pool with their speed and power.

This still happens: 'Could we get Kirsty Brown, Sam Brown, Adam Brown and Lucy Brown to the marshalling area for the 4 x 50 metre individual medley, please.' And then Mrs Brown would walk up and down and up and down the sideline with four stop watches.

I have been to many a swimming carnival. I have watched hundreds of kids throw themselves in. I have always cheered on the kid who was doing his best impersonation of Eric the Eel, and am almost reduced to tears as they just manage to get to the end before drowning.

I will never forget a particular carnival when this one kid finished his race, got out of the pool and stopped just in front of me. He leant over and unleashed the world's biggest vomit. The whole thing was done silently and, if it were not for the tremendous splash onto the pavement, it might have gone unnoticed. Those who know me understand my very sensitive gag reflex so I fled to a far-flung corner of the aquatic centre and practised my deep breathing while trying not to hurl my own cookies. My take-home lesson? DO NOT DRINK THREE CANS OF FANTA BEFORE YOU SWIM 50 METRES OF BUTTERFLY. No good can come from it.

—25—

SO FANCY

You know the stories right? About how your grandmother walked for three hours through the snow with nothing on her feet apart from a few old boxes tied up with twine to get to school? How she carried a burlap sack with a crust of bread and half an orange for her daily sustenance? And how she had to fight off savage beasts with her bare hands, before copping the cane when she eventually got to school, because she was nine seconds late?

Yeah, you know them. And it begs the question: when did it all get so fancy?

As I drop my kids at school each day, I line my car up with the others, all shiny late-model four-wheel drives what will never see a farm or the bush. Known as Toorak Tractors, they are typically Volkswagen Touaregs or BMW X5s. Well, they are where I live anyway.

In the back of these beasts are our kids, their eyes glued to the built-in DVD player all the way to kiss-and-drop zone, where they reach for school bags containing any or all of the following:

- Organic lunch in insulated container.
- Permission notes.
- A flute.
- A tennis racquet.
- Money in an envelope for an excursion to the Opera House.
- A tablet loaded with school-approved apps for learning.
- A speech about who inspires you and why printed out on little cards.
- A water bottle labelled with your kid's name.
- Birthday invitations designed by some hotshot graphic designer, containing details of your child's birthday party (a trip to a water park, then a meal at a hatted restaurant followed by a sleepover at the Hilton).
- A pencil case from Smiggle with coordinated pens, rubbers and other such crap.
- A small piece of unidentifiable rotten fruit, because it doesn't matter how fancy you are, some things never change.

Of course, this brand of fanciness is specific, not universal, and is confined to areas such as Sydney's North Shore or Eastern Suburbs, Melbourne's Toorak or, down the coast, Portsea, and Cottesloe in Perth. But that doesn't change the fact that, overall, the education system has become extremely fancy compared to what our ancestors had to contend with. Not to mention what *we* had to contend with . . .

Personally, I'm lucky to be alive, as I was a child of the Unflued Gas Heating Era. Perhaps you were as well?

Did you used to sit on those blue metal heaters in the classroom to thaw your freezing arse? Turns out, we were all being slowly poisoned by the Department of Education. Known as an unflued gas heater, that blue metal baby was in fact emitting invisible poisonous gases; nasty stuff like nitrogen dioxide, formaldehyde, carbon dioxide and that old chestnut, carbon monoxide. We were breathing in these toxic vapours all day, as we sat and rote learnt our seven times tables. As we filled in the blanks of the comprehension sheets. As we sniffed the shit out of those comprehension sheets that were fresh off the spirit duplicator. We were also sniffing the shit out of mono-fluoro tri-chloro methane and ethylene glycol monoethyl ether.

Is it any wonder that I found it hard to conquer the times tables? I was high.

There's no chance of getting carbon monoxide poisoning in the classroom these days. We have temperature-controlled climates. In fact, we have controlled everything.

There are bus monitors to monitor kids' behaviour on the bus. Library monitors to make sure things run smoothly in the library at lunchtime. There are school crossing monitors, lunch monitors, line monitors, computer room monitors, canteen monitors, sports monitors and assembly monitors. Everything that can be done in school is now monitored.

I cannot pinpoint the moment that huge, big sunhats became compulsory, although I do blame them for the lack of freckled-faced kids who now roam the modern playgrounds of our country. Only time will tell whether this practice will lower our incidence of skin cancer as they get older. Peeling, red raw noses were the rule when I was a kid, not the exception. Now, if you send your kids to school with sunburn, well you might as well send in a peanut butter sandwich as well, such is your negligence.

According to the Royal Children's Hospital in Melbourne, a child only needs six to seven minutes of direct sunlight per day to get their hit of vitamin D but, of course, only when smothered in sunscreen. If this is just not doable in your situation, you can always contribute to the billion-dollar supplement industry that is currently booming.

I remember when I was about five years old I had a pill addiction. I discovered our neighbours, the Sugdens, had a stash of fizzy vitamin C tablets that I would eat handfuls of every time I went for a visit. They kept them on a low shelf in their pantry at a time when childproof lids had not been invented. My visits to the Sugdens often ended with an explosive asshole.

But it is true that today we get our vitamin advice now from washed-out soap stars and the sister of a Hollywood actress. *Head tilt. Smiles empathetically. Holds bottle to camera. Have kids playing in the background with a dog of pure breeding.*

Or you can just cut up an orange, hand it to your children and tell them there is nothing else if greeted with protest. Better still, peg it out into the stinking hot backyard, set your timer for seven minutes and congratulate yourself on keeping it real.

— 26 —

WHAT SCHOOL MUM IS THAT?

One of the strange phenomena that happens when your kid starts primary school is that you are automatically labelled a 'school mum'.

Being a school mum can take you right back to the school playground in many ways, because, just like when you were at school yourself, there are different cliques and categories and you don't want to fall in with the wrong crowd. In this chapter, I am going to help you to identify the different types of school mum, and hopefully help to guide you through the sometimes delightful and sometimes confusing reality of being a grown-up in the school environment. (And, as usual, my musings and advice should be taken with a grain of salt, as they are served with a hefty dose of generalisation.)

SANCTIMONIOUS MUM

Sanctimonious Mum knows the name of the Unknown Soldier. She is swift to point out your shortcomings and will share her opinion on anything, whether it is asked for or not. Quite often she is highly intelligent and has based her opinions on hard facts and research.

If you disagree with her, her natural reaction would be a slight flare of the nostril, a slight head tilt and a short but meaningful death stare. It's best not to disagree with her for she is also a good gossip and can destroy you and your reputation within one canteen duty.

Teachers are frightened of the Sanctimonious Mum, for she thinks nothing of entering a classroom and demanding to know why her gifted and talented child was not chosen for the gifted and talented program. The world revolves around her needs and desires and should you dare object . . . NOSTRIL FLARE!

PURIST MUM

Purist Mum had a drug-free birth and reminds you of it often. She will bring gluten-free protein balls—homemade, naturally—into the classroom to celebrate her kid's birthday and, you wouldn't believe it, they're actually made with beetroot!

The Purist Mum is a real mover and shaker when it comes to implementing environmental projects within the school. You can bet a bunch of organic carrots that she helped set up the vegetable garden and she'll always be asking you to join her co-op. She wears a wide-brimmed hat and no makeup, and is the picture of sunny, smiling health. I am quite often inspired by the Purist

Mum—not enough to put down my can of Diet Coke and get into making my own kombucha, but I do find them to be an interesting and important part of the school mum mix.

WORKING MUM

The Working Mum is often a target of scorn because she is unable to go on excursions, do canteen, host play dates or drop everything to go to the cafe for a flat white and a gossip (because she is at work).

Whether she works though necessity or for sanity, the Working Mum needs the support of others in the community to make her life easier, or just possible. You rarely see her, as her kids are in before- and after-school care, but she rushes into assemblies when she can make it, always with an apologetic look, as if she obliged to justify her choices. And of course she shouldn't have to.

I have been the Working Mum. I know how difficult it can be. I know the guilt and I also recall the loveliness of those other mothers who would help me out when things got a bit too crazy.

SLACKER MUM

All hail the Slacker Mum, who is slack. But guess what? She just doesn't care! Her anxiety levels are very low and things happen at her pace. So she might not be great at handing in notes. Her kids' books remain contact-free long after Easter has come and gone. She may or may not turn up to reading groups that week, depending on her mood.

The Slacker Mum often orders her kids' lunches at the canteen because she has forgotten to buy bread. The Slacker Mum sends her kids to school in their normal uniform on mufti days, because she never got around to reading the school newsletter. It is not unusual to see the Slacker Mum at the school gate in her pyjama pants, sans bra and with her hair unbrushed. Judge away if you want, but she is just getting on with getting on, and doesn't care what you think.

GETS-SHIT-DONE MUM

Every school needs a smattering of these women. They are essential for a school to keep ticking over. Some other mums are fearful of them and their formidable organisational skills, but you shouldn't shrink away; you should be bloody thankful to have them in your playground.

How else would you get a pink mug on Mother's Day that says WORLD'S GREATEST MUM, if not for the Get-Shit-Done Mum who organised the stall? These mums arrange for thoughtful gifts to be given to the teacher on their birthday and at Christmas time. They are inevitably the 'class mum' who will coordinate communications for important events, such as class dinners and park dates.

I love Get-Shit-Done Mums. They keep me honest and tell me when I have forgotten to send in a box of tissues or something equally random. In fact, I have befriended a Get-Shit-Done Mum who now thoughtfully texts me important reminders as described in a previous chapter. ☺

As I said earlier, you might find this type of mum intimidating, but I urge you to embrace her. She has a genuine desire to help—to GET SHIT DONE. And, hey, if she wasn't there, then you might have to do it. Think about it.

TOO-COOL MUM

Well, quite frankly, the Too-Cool Mums frighten the bejesus out of me. They walk as if they have never tripped over a tree root in their life, and they can do it while drinking coffee at the same time as checking their phone. They don't even have to look where they are going. It is like their brains are pre-programmed to avoid things that might trip them.

Do I sound like I am a little in awe of them? Yes, perhaps I am. Once, I even tried to be one.

My oldest son had started kindy and I befriended the coolest mum I had ever seen. And guess what? SHE LIKED ME! She really, really liked me! So I did what any woman with low self-esteem does: I tried to be someone that I was not. I tried to be 'fashion forward'.

Suddenly I was taking an interest in what was considered 'trendy' at the time. I spent hours tracking down cool things I'd seen in magazines. We would have conversations in the play-ground about the merits of my handbag. This went on for a few months, and then a military jacket caused me to take a good, hard look at myself.

The military trend was everywhere, so of course I bought a black jacket adorned with so much braid and bling that I looked like I had come straight from the photo shoot for the *Sergeant Pepper* album cover.

I wore it to school pick-up and waited breathlessly for my cool friend's praise. And, well . . . she said nothing. She didn't even acknowledge that she was sitting next to a military (quasi) official. I mean, I wasn't expecting a salute or anything, just some sort of acknowledgment of how cool I was.

And then it hit me. This girl wasn't fashion forward at all! She just had a really cool style. She didn't march to the military beat of someone else's drum; she was just born cool. And once I realised this, my days of being fashion forward were discarded as quickly as a pair of poop-catcher pants into a Vinnie's bag.

For I am not a cool mum. And I am okay with that.

TIGER MUM

In 2011 Chinese American mum Amy Chua published a book called *Battle Hymn of the Tiger Mother*, and all of a sudden this tribe had a name. Tiger Mums are, in essence, totally devoted to their kids and are determined that they will achieve 110 per cent of their potential, come hell or high water.

The children of Tiger Mums are required to be fluent in many languages, to play a musical instrument with the proficiency of a professional musician and to attain brilliant academic results with ease.

I myself have encountered an actual Tiger Mum. Two in fact.

The first encounter with a Tiger Mum occurred over a ballet bun. I said I could take her daughter, along with my son, to their weekly ballet class. She agreed that this would be okay. She later called to ask me about my competence when it comes to scraping hair up into a bun. My mistake was to pause for a moment as my brain took a while to comprehend what she was asking. She took this silence as a weakness when it came to my hairdressing ability so my offer of help was rescinded.

The next Tiger Mum was far more brutal.

She had identified that one of my kids had a natural affinity with a tennis racquet and asked whether he might be interested in partnering her son in an upcoming tournament. I could see no reason why not, although he had never played in a tournament before and I had no idea what that might entail. I just thought it was a chance for him to get out on a court and have a hit. They're just having fun, right?

Wrong. It was far more serious than that. The Tiger Mum handed me a practice schedule and made it clear that she expected us to follow it. (This might be a good time to mention that, at the time, my son was eight.)

After a fortnight of practice, Tiger Mum informed me that I needed to get my son a new racquet—this afternoon, preferably, as they needed to practice in the morning.

I should have told her to fuck off then and there, but she was scary.

So to cut a long story short, a new racquet was purchased and our sons went on to place third in the tournament.

Tiger Mum was gutted. 'You didn't give him enough time to get used to his new racquet!' she cried.

I nodded in agreement, then left. As soon as I reached the car, I deleted her number from my phone.

Never again. Roar in someone else's direction, thank you very much.

PERFECT MUM

The Perfect Mum is a fictional character who only exists in margarine ads. You know the type, don't you? Advertisers would have us believe that all mums get around with perfect blow-dries, straight shiny teeth and wearing expensive linen. She is inevitably a truly content stay-at-home Mum and almost always has a golden retriever that springs from the car when she goes to unpack the shopping.

Her kids sit up nicely at the bench in her sparkling kitchen, as she presents them with something freshly baked, at the sight of which they declare that she is the best mum in Australia, if not the world.

The Perfect Mum will smile her perfect smile, then reach for some sort of pre-packaged, pre-moistened antibacterial towelette to wipe up some invisible crumbs. After which, together with her cherubs, she will open the dishwasher so everyone can admire how clean it is.

The Perfect Mum also takes fibre tablets and uses incontinence pads when she jumps on the trampoline, which she seems to do often.

And now let me reiterate: THE PERFECT MUM DOES NOT EXIST.

*

Every mum has her strengths and weaknesses, every mum suffers her highs and lows. A lot of us look at other mums and think, 'I don't know how she does it.' But the truth of the matter is, nobody does it by the book.

Because there is no book.

Actually, I stand corrected. There are a million books on mothering.

Okay, not quite a million. According to Amazon, there are 137,464 titles on mothering available for you to order today, and with such fascinating titles on offer, why wouldn't you clog up your noggin with ridiculous fluff? Choose from:

Mothering with Purpose: Winning the heart of your child
The Zen Mother Made Easy!

The Peaceful Mom: How to stop yelling
The Guide to Meaningful and Significant Mothering

The truth is, these books are full of bullshit.

The truth is, we need all of the types of mums—the ones outlined in this chapter and many more besides.

The truth is, no matter what you are doing, someone will think you are doing it wrong. So learn to be cool with that.

Now, can I interest you in a large floral headband? Or perhaps some camouflage pants?

THE MOTHER'S DAY STALL

There have been a motley collection of Mother's and Father's Day gifts from school stalls over the years, but none so fabulous as those described in this anecdote:

> At dawn one Mother's Day my eight-year-old son presented me with a still life of a phallic gourd, a pair of acrylic exfoliating gloves and some tissues decorated with animals. 'Good luck with getting the snot on the animals!' he enthusiastically declared. His younger sister gave me a little tin bucket with lollies—'Mum, can I have the lollies, and you can use the bucket to carry sand at the beach! You can even poo into it!' By this time I was half crying, half laughing, my

sleep-addled brain full of an image of myself
scrubbing off dead skin cells then shitting into
a bucket the size of a teacup! At least I didn't get
the bottle of toilet cleaner the ladies at the school
Mother's Day stall were apparently selling . . .

—27—

THE (SCHOOL) TIE THAT BINDS

Studies have shown that students from private schools are more likely to get into uni and end up making a lot more money; while wife-beaters and rapists are nearly all public-school-educated. Sorry, no offence, but it's true.

JA'MIE KING

Once upon a time there was a young girl who lived on the outskirts of the Sydney suburban sprawl in an area that was well known for superior marijuana cultivation. As the girl was finishing her primary school education, her parents became concerned that she would fall in with the wrong crowd, for she was a wild child in the making.

Her bedroom walls were lined with posters of Brian Mannix, Pseudo Echo and a strung out Michael Hutchence, and when she was sprung smoking Winfield Reds with her friend Audra and word came back about her kissing episodes, the decision was made.

'You, young lady, are going to boarding school!' her parents announced one night over dinner.

The girl gently put her knife and fork down, then unleashed a string of expletives unlike anything her parents had ever heard and which only hardened their resolve. So, kicking and screaming, she was packed up and deposited on the steps of a high-falutin', fancy all-girls school, which opened up a whole new world to her.

This world was governed by fantastic teachers by day, and at night by pill-popping, depressed boarding house mistresses who were unaware that their fifteen-year-old charges were stealing away in the middle of the night, taking the train into the city and dancing with American sailors at dirty bars in Kings Cross.

This behaviour continued for years, and while she saw her peers expelled for all sorts of shenanigans, her street smarts ensured she was never caught. She became a fabulous liar, so convincing that it was thought she might have a future career treading the boards.

There were some close calls, of course, such as the morning when she woke up snuggled next to her boyfriend in the boarding house. The housemistress banged on the door loudly, almost causing said boyfriend to defecate. He ducked under the doona, while our heroine and the housemistress had a short but heated argument as to why she was not attending chapel, repenting her sins.

As the end of her schooling drew closer, her parents became anxious with regards to her final results, as well they might. The word 'horrified' might have been used. The term 'waste of money' was definitely uttered.

'What went wrong?' they asked each other. 'We sent her to a high-falutin', fancy all-girls school. We sent her to a *private* school.'

✳

The age-old debate regarding private school versus public school is still a hot topic. You'll hear it discussed wherever the parents of school-age children gather. On the sidelines of children's sporting matches. At boring dinner parties with work colleagues. At church. At rehab centres. At school gates all over the world.

'Where are your kids going to go to high school?'

Please . . . punch me in the face.

Where I live, conversation at the school gate follows a well-worn path:

'Did you do anything nice on the weekend?'

'Did Hugo/Isabella enjoy rugby/drama this week?'

'My neighbour's place went for more than two million dollars!'

'I just use sunscreen every day.'

'Where are you going skiing this year?'

'He just could not get away from the office, so I thought screw you: I'm taking the kids to Fiji for Easter.'

'So, where are you sending your boys to high school?'

Punch me in the face.

But I wasn't always so blasé on the subject of my sons' future schooling. When I was pregnant with my first son, my panic button got stuck and I was concerned about everything! So I projected my anxiety forward by . . . let's say twelve years . . . and I filled out a form to put our son on the waiting list for a fancy private school. Mr Woog begrudgingly attached a cheque to this form ten minutes after his birth and sent it off.

Then we waited, like we had paid to do. *Paid*, to be on a *waiting list*. In hindsight, what the fuck?

Another son came along a few years later. Again, we filled out the form, attached the cheque. Posted it.

And waited.

And then forgot about it.

A few years later, I was starting to wonder about my investment. Especially when my good friend Mrs Finlay received a confirmation letter for her son, who was a year younger than my youngest.

I called the bursar of the fancy educational establishment on Sydney's Lower North Shore. The conversation went a little something like this:

'Hi, Mrs Bursar. My name is Mrs Woog. I'm just following up on the application forms I sent in for my two kids a few years ago.'

'What are their names?'

The information was given. I was a bit frightened at this point, and was trying to be very civil and agreeable.

'We sent in our waiting-list application and fee within a week of their birth and I have not heard anything since, so I thought I'd just give you a buzz and see how the whole process is coming along. I'm so sorry to bother you; I know you must get hounded all the time. But you see—'

'Mrs Woog, we give preference to the sons of old boys and beneficiaries. I am looking at your file now and I can see that your family is neither. I'm sorry to say it's unlikely we will be offering your sons a place here.'

I will not go into detail regarding the ensuing exchange, but if I say 'you can stick your waiting list' and 'arse' and 'fascist factory', you'll probably get my drift.

As we then acknowledged our differences during our farewells, I could distinctly hear in the background the big red pen go through our names on that bloody waiting list. I can only assume that this school was perfectly happy to take my non-refundable application fee of $800 in the full knowledge that my kids had a snowball's chance in hell of ever donning their straw boater.

You must admit, this is pretty bad form.

But fate works in mysterious ways, I do believe, for not long after this I heard that the offending school had sent home letters with their students, begging the mothers of these boys not to wear gym clothes when dropping off their sons at school. What the hell? No one will tell me to take off my stretchy pants!

There are many misconceptions about private school education. One is that the students are all born with silver spoons in their mouths. The truth is, however, that many parents make huge sacrifices in order to pay the fees for six years of high school education at a private school, which may add up to as much as $180,000. In many cases, both parents will work two jobs to make sure that the bill gets paid (and, let me add, that $180,000 doesn't include the $450 you're up for each time your kid needs a new blazer).

You could say that the whole issue of public versus private comes down to a question of choice, but let's be honest: most people do not have that luxury. And does it really matter? There's a general belief that a private school education will open doors to you for the rest of your life. This might have been true even as recently as a generation ago, but the world is different now, and employers are far more focused on actual skills than on the old-boy school tie.

I will never forget talking with a career counsellor in my final year of wagging school. She actually told me that if I was competing for a job and it came down to a choice between me and another candidate, and my competitor had attended a public school, the fact that I had attended a private school would tip me into the job.

I remember being faintly horrified at this assumption of entitlement; it has left a revolting taste in my mouth to this day. At the time, it seemed that society really believed that if you attended a private school, you were a better person. A superior person. And one of the things I noticed after graduation was that these students then tended to stick together throughout the rest of their lives.

A lot of private school students never really break free from their social circle. They go to university together. They marry people who are from a similar background. They are each other's best men and bridesmaids and they end up back in the suburb that they themselves grew up in. Naturally, their children go to the same school they went to. And so the cycle continues. There is, however, a comfort in the familiar. Private schools certainly have the community spirit to their advantage, as well as time-honoured traditions.

PRIVATE OR PUBLIC?

I asked parents from across the country why they chose public or private schools for their kids, and here is what a few of them had to say:

> My daughter goes to a private school—and it's primarily due to the extra support she receives. As a child on the autistic spectrum, she would be an unfunded, unsupported student at the local public school; however, she's supported 100 per cent of the time with an aide at the school she's at. There are smaller classes and a very flexible, personalised curriculum which is tailored to highlight her strengths and provide extra support for the areas she finds challenging also helped sway us. Best decision we ever made.

> My kids struggled at state school; they hated school and didn't do well. We moved them to a private school three years ago and they are thriving. My son—who I'd always said would never be academic (he is a natural sportsman) and did really badly through to end of Year 5 in public system—is now in Year 8 and loves school. He loves learning and has improved to being a high C, low B student (even a couple of As. WHAT?!?!). He can't wait to go to uni! I hate paying the fees and, yes, it is a struggle, but the

results for us have been worth it. I feel like their future is a bit brighter because they are gaining more from their education.

Mine are all private-school educated, although my husband and I were public-school kids. Our main reason initially was related to access to an excellent music department and the strong academic focus in the school they attend. The local public schools don't have the same track record. Fortunately, it's been an excellent choice for all three kids.

I liked the uniform . . .

My girls go to a private Jewish school because I want them to learn about their culture. It's a gorgeous school and they're very happy there. I am extremely grateful to have that choice.

We've sent our boys to private school (since kindergarten) because of the small class sizes, additional teachers in the classroom most of the time, and specialist teachers for music, art and science. There are free periods for class teachers to be in contact with parents via face to face or email, regular individual support for academics if required, in addition to the fact that phone calls and emails to teacher are responded to before the end of the day.

We've done both. We've been to three different schools in five years due to moving house. School quality comes down to the leadership team. You get that right, and the rest follows, public or private.

While everyone has a different opinion, mine go public and I wouldn't ever consider private school. But I can say that because our local zoned high school is a cracker. But the most important thing for your kid—in my view and it's supported by loads of research—is having engaged parents in your education. None of the extracurricular activities and nice lawns provided by private schools will matter if your kid turns into an entitled pain in the whatsit. And for those who go private because their kids have a special need, this is completely why Gonski should be supported 100 per cent—so there is needs-based funding. Not everyone has the ways and means for this support but I totally get why, if you can afford it, that you'd do it.

The truth is that there's no such thing as a perfect educational system. Private schools and public schools—they both have their drawbacks and benefits. Let's just be grateful that there is a system for everyone.

But then again . . . what about those homeschool weirdoes? Shall we discuss them while we're at it?

YOU DO WHAT? LET'S CHAT TO A HOMESCHOOLER

Homeschooling. It is when you shun the traditional place of education, roll up your sleeves and get on with the job yourself. In Australia just decades ago it was only the deeply religious who homeschooled their young.

These days, it is become much more mainstream.

I want you to meet my friend Shae. Shae believes in feminism, real food, home education, kids with high functioning Autism Spectrum Disorder, radical homemaking, travel with kids, body positivity, connected parenting, homebirth and art. She is also one of the coolest mammas I know.

Sure, she drinks kombucha, but more often than not it is flavoured with vodka.

So, we got chatting . . .

Why did you decide that homeschooling was for your kids?

We had always planned to send our kids to a non-traditional type of school because we are not a good fit for public, mainstream school. I knew that I'd be THAT mother down at the office arguing over why we were not going to make our child do homework or why we didn't need permission from the school to take our kids out to go camping or why I couldn't get my seven-year-old out of gumboots.

212

And I was pretty sure I'd fail at five whole days in a row of clean school uniform. We had looked into Steiner and were put off by the hardcore rules.

We are a pretty laid-back kind of family. The kids have always slept without 'training' and our form of discipline didn't involve sticker charts and punishments. This meant we weren't keen to change our way of parenting when the kids turned five to include a lot of rules and restrictions about things we didn't necessarily agree with.

Through other hippy-la-la type groups we knew a couple of other families that had chosen not to send their kids to school. The kids were awesome and were always off doing cool and interesting things with lots of other families. The flexibility and amount of time the kids had to play and explore their interests was really appealing.

As was the idea of not needing to be somewhere five days a week at BOTH 9 am and 3 pm.

The year my firstborn was supposed to start four-year-old kinder was also the year I gave birth to my third child. So I had a newborn, a twenty-month-old and a just-turned four-year-old and I was barely able to have a shower. I was not interested in changing the routine we had that already included lots of great stuff and, surprisingly to some, lots of other people.

So we opted out of kinder and, as the year wore on, I could see how what we were doing was working for everyone. So we decided to opt out of prep and see how it went.

It was a success and now the more years we are out of the school system with our three kids, the less appealing that system is.

My kids have been able to learn on their own schedule, about things that interest them, in a way that suits their learning style. They can jump years ahead or be behind their peers and it doesn't matter. We go on excursions, camps, park meet-ups, and play dates. We have heaps of time for extracurricular activities, classes or tutoring.

And not a school run in sight.

It's not for everyone, but it really works for us.

What are some of the common misconceptions people make about homeschooling?

That all the kids are weird, gifted, wild, like Laura from *Little House on the Prairie*, and all the adults are religious, rich, hippies or like Caroline from *Little House on the Prairie*. The reality is that homeschooled families are as likely to be religious as they are atheist, and you can meet as many Lukes as you do Phoenixes.

There are rich, working-class and single-parent families. Some replicate school at home and some unschool. Homeschooling is a great option for gifted and special needs kids, and lots of families also choose it for their perfectly ordinary or not academic kids too. The home education community in Australia is a diverse melting pot with a bit of everything.

Despite people often asking me this when we are out in social situations, the most common misconception is that homeschooled kids are missing out socially. School is one way to socialise (even though every teacher I ever had told me I was NOT there to do that), but not the only way.

Do you ever think your kid is going to suddenly lose the ability to talk to their peers over the school holidays because there is no school? No. You take them out; you catch up with friends. And with the number of home-educated kids on the rise it's only getting easier.

What does a typical day look like for you and your kids?

We all wake up at different times and like a slow start. I don't answer any questions until after my cup of tea at around 8.30 am.

If it's a day at home with no plans, the computers or devices or the TV usually get a red-hot go until about 10 am. We just take the rest of the day as it comes. Before lunch the kids might make some art or work on their project books, we might hit the library or go to the park.

I keep a mental list of subjects the kids are interested or currently immersed in and I might show them a documentary or YouTube video, or read and explain something about or from a reference book, or we might do an experiment or go on an excursion. If the kids are working on something that requires a lot of practice, then we aim to do this in the morning.

After lunch the kids mostly play.

Sometimes it's messy, sometimes it's outside, and often it's loud and includes arguments. Now that the kids are older, I am usually only needed to help get stuff down from high places, answer questions, and tie up Monster High hair, so I usually do my own stuff all arvo (read my Kindle and look at Pinterest), as well as catching up on housework and cooking dinner.

Hubs arrives home at about 6 pm and after dinner we might play card or board games or watch TV or a movie. That's a cruisey day without activities though. My kids all do dancing, one does swimming, and the other two do drama. We also go to one or two home education park meet-ups a week, as well as various play dates and day trips or excursions around the place.

The 'homeschool' stuff just fits in around the activities and general life. Learning happens all the time.

What are some of the disadvantages to homeschooling?

That anytime your child is anything less than extraordinary, perfectly behaved, blissfully joyous and completely outgoing then someone will always tell you to send them to school to 'fix' your problem.

Kids can be sobbing every morning at school drop-off or needing to see a psychologist because of bullying and parents are told that 'school is tough', but have one shitty homeschooling day and it's like you brought it on yourself. It's also incredibly frustrating for kids to feel like they have to be on their best behaviour at all times or be judged. I think my kids are amazing, but they shouldn't be held up to a higher standard.

For me, the driving around is a big one. School is usually local and comes with a local posse of kids and families that become part of your 'tribe'. The homeschool community can be a bit far-flung so your kids might end up chumming up with not-so-local friends. The excursions are also not a matter of signing a form and the kids being bussed from said local school. We drive to stuff that's interesting and sometimes, if there is a lot on, it can mean many hours in the car.

Does homeschooling ever drive you to drink? How do you manage all that together time?

The bits that drive me to drink are pretty much the same as for a lot of school parents: fighting kids, grocery shopping, the backseat of my car being like a garbage dump.

We're all not so different really.

There are lots of ways to home-educate your kids but I think the one that pops into most people's minds is the model of 'school at home'; for example, a parent sitting at a table with their kids for five or so hours a day, trying to get them to do worksheets and memorise times tables. Then after the schoolwork is finished the kids don't know how to spend their time unless an adult (the homeschooling parent) is telling them what to do and is constantly involved in all their activities.

The truth is that parents who follow full curriculum only need to do a couple to a few hours of bookwork a day, and most do less than that. Once kids are competent readers then they can be set up with projects and workbooks, needing only small amounts of parental involvement here and there. Many homeschooling families (like ours) take a much more laid-back approach and it is mostly driven by the kids themselves, with help where needed.

I understand that people think that the learning part is full-on, hands-on hours and hours a day— but it really isn't like that. Although I have been needed to explain things like the difference between continents and cities and countries first thing in the morning or the solar system last thing at night. That CAN be exhausting.

As far as together time, that is less intense than you might think as well. I'm sure people think it's lots of I'M BORED and being asked to play dinosaurs or hearing about Minecraft all day long (okay, you will actually hear A LOT about Minecraft) but, for me, it's tapered off as the kids have gotten older. One of the great things about opting out of school is opting out of kids being kept busy all the time.

Free time makes them resourceful, happy to potter around and amuse themselves. I can go actual hours without any of my children wanting me to be involved in a thing. Of course the flipside is that some days are really intense and everyone wants me to watch, help out, answer questions, mediate, etc., all while I really need to go shopping and no one wants to go. But it seems to balance itself out.

I personally have a local mother-in-law who takes the kids for school hours one day a week. I know families who use nannies or child care so they have a bit of kid-free time or an opportunity to get a haircut without taking four kids along.

The truth is I love the together time. I know I'm supposed to love it when they are out of my hair, but I sure like having them around now.

You can follow Shae's adventures by reading her blog @ freerangeinsuburbia.com.

28

THE DOG ATE MY HOMEWORK

'Mum, what is the quotient of 7 and 63?'

Have you ever had your kid ask you a question like this? By which I mean: you have absolutely no idea what they're talking about? So you google *quotient* and Wikipedia hits you up with this:

In mathematics, a quotient (from Latin: quotiens 'how many times', pronounced ˈkwoʊʃənt) is the result of division. [1] For example, when dividing 6 by 3, the quotient is 2, while 6 is called the dividend, and 3 the divisor. The quotient further is expressed as the number of times the divisor divides into the dividend, e.g. 3 divides 2 times into 6. A quotient can also mean just the integer part of the result of dividing two integers. For example, the quotient of 13 divided by 5 would be 2 while the remainder would be 3. For more, see the Euclidean division.

And then you're left standing there, absentmindedly scratching the inside of your ear, before saying something along the lines of '. . . Division? Or something related to dividing things?'

It is true that there are many occasions when my offspring have proven to be smarter than me, especially when it comes to using the Foxtel remote or certain social media apps. But it's a little disconcerting when I am unable to do Year 5 maths—especially considering that, at one stage, I was in charge of teaching it!

It seems that, with age, my brain has turned to ham-and-pea soup, and I now struggle with the basic elements of reading, writing and arithmetic.

I recall getting my first gold star in class. My heart almost burst such was my immense pride. I can even still remember why I got it: I was able to demonstrate, using my pointer finger, the hidden number 2, which was disguised as half of an angel. Miss Babos and I, we were such a great team. Finding hidden numbers, lining up our Cuisenaire rods, playing games with counters. Now *that* is my idea of maths, and I'm fairly sure I'd still be able to find that hidden number 2 today. But at some point—and I think it's from about Year 3—maths goes from Johnny having four apples and Beth having five and how many do they have altogether to 'Is 70,173,454 divisible by 5?'. It's a bit like playing 'Chopsticks' on the piano and then, moments later, being asked to play Chopin's Piano Concerto no. 3 in A major in front of a packed concert hall. There is a huge gap that causes a disconnect. And it is at the precise moment when your child writes 'yes' in answer to the question about 70,173,454 that you realise your kid is smarter than you.

Debate has raged over the decades as to whether homework is beneficial at all. When yours truly was at school, we had a list of ten spelling words that we had to learn during the week. We were tested on these words each Friday, and if you got all ten correct, you were the lucky recipient of jelly snake. Wow! That was all the incentive I needed to ensure that, come Friday, I was down with that list.

The hours after school were spent exploring the neighbourhood on our bikes, playing cricket on the road, or trying to avoid being pummelled by that evil Benny Brown who lived on the next street.

So, when did homework creep in? Why are we now faced with *more* things to do after school? How do we fit it in around footy practice, ballet, Mandarin, tennis lessons, judo, organic smoothie-making masterclasses, touch-typing lessons, maths tutoring and crafternoons? Do we expect our kids to do their maths homework while in the waiting room of the dentist/dermatologist/allergist/podiatrist/physiotherapist/kinesiologist?

And why do I have to be the big mean mummy overseeing all of these extra activities?

'Have you done your homework?' I ask each day, and each day comes the reply: 'Yes.'

On further investigation, it is revealed that the homework is actually still in the school bag, untouched, and the whole lot is due tomorrow.

And just what are these fucking complex sentences of which you speak? What the hell is an independent clause? A subordinating conjunction? Surely these terms belong in a courtroom, not on page 40 of Lauren O'Brien and John Walters' *Grammar Conventions: National Grammar and Language Activities for Grade 6*, 2nd edition.

This book will also familiarise your child with modality, adverbials, cohesive devices and an anxiety disorder. Now, I am far from being on the invitation list for Mensa, but I have racked my brain recalling my own school days, and all I can remember is the spelling list. And times tables. That's about it. (Apart from sport and library, which of course were my favourite part of the school curriculum, other than big lunch and little lunch.)

But education is different these days, and schools are expected to develop homework policies that cater to the particular needs of their children. When teachers give homework, it's not because they're sadists; it's because, generally speaking, teachers are good people who want to see your lovely kids succeed. Homework is important to establish good study habits, to extend the learning done in the classroom and to enforce self-discipline. (Which I think is a lot to ask of a five-year-old who just wants to pick his nose, roll it up into a ball and flick it at his brother.) Teachers rejoice in seeing their students overcome learning obstacles, develop problem-solving skills and reach academic milestones. But don't forget, homework is a pain in the arse for them too, because they have to mark every page and write some sort of encouraging comment for every kid. And mostly they have to do it on the weekend.

Thanks to all this homework, we are producing a new breed of super-smart kids, but I for one am bloody useless when it comes to helping them out. And I believe there does come a point when your personal pride should be placed above grammar conventions and obtuse angles, so I am happy to provide you with a template that you can print off and send to your school should all this homework palaver get too much:

Dear Sir or Madam,

    This CEASE AND DESIST ORDER is to inform you that your harassing and intimidating actions are completely unacceptable and will not be tolerated in any way, shape or form. Should you continue to pursue these brain-zapping activities in violation of this CEASE AND DESIST ORDER, I will not hesitate to pursue further legal action against you, including, but not limited to, civil action and/or criminal complaints.

I have had to pull a very comprehensive report about the Daintree Rainforest out of my arse in less than twenty-four hours.

I still don't know how to spell conscieous/conscience/conchous without having to resort to spellcheck, yet it seems to be on the kids' spelling list every week. Ditto definantly/defenently.

I keep confusing Modality with some sort of feminine hygiene product.

Fridays roll around far too quickly and I find it very taxing to finish the homework on time. I can never seem to find a blue pen, so my kid does his homework in black pen, and then you write a comment on the homework stressing that he is required to use blue pen, yet you write it in RED!

The advanced nature of the work required of my eleven-year-old makes me question my own mental capacities, which in turn causes my self-confidence to suffer. I do not enjoy it when my kids soundly demonstrate superior mental computation strategies by adding up complex numbers just by using their brain, while I have to write down sums and carry numbers and all that crap. When doing or discussing homework with my kids, I feel a mix of shame and stupidity.

Please note that I have the right to remain free from your intimidating homework tactics, and I intend to protect that right. Note that a copy of this letter and a record of its delivery will be stored. Note too that it is admissible as evidence in a court of law and will be used should the need arise in the future.

This CEASE AND DESIST ORDER demands that you immediately discontinue and do not at any point henceforth do the following to me: highlight my lack of basic skills in numeracy and literacy; put red frowny faces on my work; put red question marks on my work; or send me a note saying that my work is not up to the class standard.

Failure to comply with my demands will send me to the nearest bottle of gin, whereupon I will be forced to remove the lid and have a big swig. And because the gin is almost 100% defiantly going to make me cry, you will have that on your conscience as well.

Given that homework seems to be a necessary evil, let us now take a look at some of the excuses one might use to get out of submitting one's homework, and common teacher responses.

I forgot my homework. No shit? You just haven't done it.

I didn't know it was due today. Of course you knew it was due today, because it is Friday and that's the day that you wear your sports uniform and it is also the day that you get a lunch order because your useless mother has run out of bread. And fruit. And anything else that could be identified as sustenance. You just haven't done your homework.

Start crying. This one has its advantages. Depending on the type of teacher you have, this can be a very effective way of getting out of your homework. It's particularly good if you can manage to get yourself worked up into an advanced state of hysteria, with uncontrollable snot issues and perhaps a cheeky stint of hyperventilation. Chances are you will be sent to the sick bay to calm the fuck down.

I accidentally threw it out. What? You threw out two large textbooks, your iPad and an additional green plastic portfolio? Don't take me for a fool, young lady.

Mum was too busy watching YouTube clips of Tatum Channing with his shirt off and couldn't help me. Embarrassing, but credible.

The dog ate my homework. Everyone has used this excuse in some point in their life, even if they have never owned a dog. Because it cannot be proven, you may get away with this once. But keep it up your sleeve. Don't go in too hard with this one too early in the year.

And even if coming up with excuses is the only way you can help your children with their homework, as ever, try to ensure that the excuses sound like the kids' own work.

29

PLEASE REPORT TO THE OFFICE

The most hideous war in human history—the Drug War—
is being fought throughout the world at this moment.
Its devastation reaches Australia. It is a war without
honour. No monuments list the dead, the wounded, and
the innocent victims. Daily the number of casualties, daily
the number of deaths, increases more rapidly.

REVEREND TED NOFFS

In 1974 the Reverend Ted Noffs and his wife Margaret established the Life Education Centre to help inform children about
the dangers of drugs. Mobile classrooms are parked in schools
around the country to help deliver the anti-drugs message. So
when the note came home that Healthy Harold was coming to
our hood, I signed that piece of paper giving permission for my
kids to be taught about the evils of drugs.

Then word came through that some of the kids had caught the Healthy Harold lady smoking behind the van. The principal was alerted and Mrs Healthy Harold was warned not to smoke on school property anymore. It was the most scandalous thing that had happened in our suburb since some brain surgeon wrote FUK on the side of the IGA with spray paint.

School visitors are nothing new. One of my own most vivid memories involves a lady coming in to talk to us about Dr Barnardo's Homes. It was the late 1970s and this striking-looking lady with the biggest afro I have ever seen came through the door of the classroom and took her place in the circle. (We were, of course, on the floor, while she took a seat on a chair.) And when she opened her mouth to speak, well, she sounded like she had walked straight off the set of a movie.

For she was an American! A real-life American! And so I hung on her every word. She told us a story about Dr Barnardo, who lived in London, and how he was horrified by the number of homeless children living on the street. So he opened homes to house the kids.

By all accounts Dr Barnardo was a very nice man who did very good works. But that's not why I remember the details of Dr Barnardo's Homes all these years later. No, it's because of the exotic visitor to our classroom who spent thirty minutes hypnotising us.

'Dr. Barnado's. Homes.' She must have repeated these three words dozens of times, always with a dramatic pause between each word. 'Dr. Banardo's. Homes.'

At first, she simply asked us to repeat the words back to her.

'Dr. Barnado's. Homes,' we chorused obediently.

Then she mixed it up a little. 'Dr . . . ?'

'Barnado's. Homes,' we replied.

'And so you will ask your parents to put money into these envelopes for ... ?'

'Dr. Barnado's. Homes.'

And then she left, while we all looked at each other and wondered what the hell had just happened.

Primary schools are almost always crawling with visitors, from the plumber who's come to unblock a dunny that had been stuffed full of unwanted sandwiches to the school district superintendent who has come to assess the quality of the kindergarten class's finger-painting. But there is one thing that they all have to do: report to the office.

Every visitor to the school must sign in and declare their business. This is meant to weed out any undesirables. But some still get in.

Much like my glamorous American brainwasher, corporate businesses are keen to get in front of a large group of kids and sell them their message. Like:

If you get Mum and Dad to do their weekly shop at our super-market, and you bring all your receipts in and put them in this heavily branded box that we will provide to your school FOR FREE, then we will give your school an uninflated basketball. But remember, that's only if your school community spends $45,000 with us in the next fortnight!

Or what about the beverage company that will trot out a couple of AFL players to talk to your kids about fitness and health?

Plus, we will give you each a cheap branded sun visor and take a photo of you with said AFL player and use the image on social media! #lifeissweet

And of course there is the burger giant that gives out grants to community sporting groups with one hand, while shoving hot salty fries into your children's mouths with the other.

*

A few years ago, one of my children suffered an addiction. An addiction to jumping rope. A team of skipping professionals had been bussed in and they proceeded to put on a fantastic, artistic display of skipping. It was enough to inspire my youngest to abandon his dream of being a world-class handball player and reach for a skipping rope—and so my nightmare began.

My nightmare was fuelled by a school program sponsored by a national healthcare, financial services and retirement living organisation, providing services to more than half a million Australians and health cover to close to 300,000 Australians.

Thwack, thwack, thwack, thwack, thwack.

The noise drove me to drink. It was the first thing that I heard every morning.

Thwack, thwack, thwack, thwack, thwack.

Every afternoon after school.

Thwack, thwack, thwack, thwack, thwack.

And all day on weekends.

Thwack, thwack, thwack, thwack, thwack, thwack, thwack.

I'd had no idea a five-year-old was capable of such commitment.

And then the Jump Rope for Heart day came around, a glorious festival which culminated in a whole school skip-off. And smack me across the face with a piece of rope if my kid's class didn't triumph over all the other kindergarten classes!

So of course I was as proud as punch. My son, skipping champion. Despite the fact that he had only raised $7.15, which was the amount I happened to have on me at the time.

And while we are speaking of fundraising, whose idea was it to send kids home with a box of giant Caramello Koalas to sell? So, you get a box of forty-eight giant chocolate-covered, gooey, caramel-centred koalas, proceed to eat them all yourself, then—filled with guilt and shame—fork over $50.

But at least with the giant koala caper you are getting something for your dough. At one Sydney private school, you can pay a thousand dollars and, in return, they will give you a brick. But—here's the catch—they don't actually give it to you. They use it to make a walking path. Now, I would never stand accused of being an astute businessperson, but even I can tell that a thousand bucks for one brick offers a very poor return on my investment.

Another visitor to my primary school was a dental nurse. She would set up in a small demountable and the children then lined up at the door. One by one, our teacher would usher us in. The nurse would ask us to open our mouths, and she would have a little look around. If you got a note to take home, it meant that you had a cavity and needed to go to the dentist. If not, you were good to go.

I didn't get the note of doom, but I was rewarded with a liberal dose of a gross pink slime—fluoride, apparently—and I can still remember the taste vividly all these decades later. It was so offensive it brought several kids to tears. But that was nothing compared to what happened to you in Year 6 . . .

If you were a girl in Year 6, there was a vial of rubella vaccination with your name on it somewhere. We were all lined up and sent into the demountable one by one. There, the doctor came at us with a needle: JAB! There was much dramatic wailing afterwards, so if you were at the end of the queue, because your surname started with a letter at the end of the alphabet, you were completely traumatised by the time it was your turn.

But there were good visitors as well.

Like when the reptile man would come to town, laden with turtles and snakes for us to look at. I remember the delicious frisson of terror I felt as he explained how venomous the snakes were.

And then there was the day that the government realised too many kids were being badly injured when riding their bikes to school, so they asked Molly Meldrum—who was everyone's hero at the time, because he had recently interviewed a young Madonna—to endorse the Stackhat. And, boy, did this endorsement lead to sales! When the Stackhat was first introduced to the market in 1982, it was sold at a few bike shops but not in any head-turning numbers. By 1986, two million kids were riding the suburbs of Australia with their heads protected by Stackhats. Despite the fact that the helmet weighed about twenty-five kilograms and was Lego yellow, and thus was neither attractive nor comfortable, sales soared.

Our school immediately placed a bulk order for Stackhats and instituted a policy whereby all children who rode a bike to school must be wearing one. And because there was always a reason to celebrate a mandatory policy, we had a special Bike Day with a representative from Stackhat on hand to show us how to put on a bike helmet. (Clearly we must have been considered deadly stupid.)

I can't say that Bike Day was a raging success. To begin with, because this was the day on which the Stackhats were to be given out, we all had to walk our bikes to school, as we were no longer allowed to ride lid-free. Then, once we were given our Stackhats, mayhem ensued. Face it, if you put 200 or so kids in clunky hats they are not used to and encourage them to ride around a fairly small area of concrete, you're just asking for trouble.

There were many, many accidents.

Luckily, we were all wearing Stackhats.

And then there were the school visitors who caused the most chaos ever.

Billets.

A call would go out from the school to let everyone know that a busload of kids were coming into town to attend some sporting event. Would anyone be prepared to host one of the visiting kids for a few nights?

You didn't need a police check, or a working with children check. All you needed was a signature and a spare couch. Looking back on it—and it still goes on—the whole notion is fraught with bad possibilities.

My mum never volunteered to billet anyone; she is a very smart woman. Now that I am a parent, I totally get it. Looking after someone else's kid is okay, but it was a bit of a lottery as to who might turn up at the door. At the time, though, I was very pissed off about it, because all my mates now had instant live-in best friends and I was stuck with my bitchy sister and my annoying brother.

The billets were always granted instant celebrity status, and my lucky school friends who were matched with the very coolest of the billet kids would ride that wave of coolness by association for all it was worth.

I'm sure having some kid from Walgett staying would have made my life richer.

—30—

PROGRAMMING THE PERFECT CHILD

> You and your child are invited to an information evening for all 1012 prospective new band members, to take place in the school hall on Tuesday at 6.30 pm. This is an important occasion and both the Junior Band and the Concert Band will be performing for you.

My immediate thought: 'How the fuck am I going to get out of this one?'

Extracurricular activities are important for a child's development as a well-rounded person; I know this, and I am all for them. But I have imposed a strict limit of two activities. The only mandatory activity is swimming lessons. I see this as a life insurance policy.

Ask any of your mates, 'How are you?', and I guarantee that they will answer: 'Busy.'

235

It starts when your baby is born. You get busy. Busy trying to get out of the house so you can cure your loneliness by meeting with a group of other mothers, known as a mothers' group. This is a bunch of women with whom you have only one thing in common: that you all enjoyed a root at roughly the same time. You spend your time at mothers' group discussing how busy you are.

As your baby grows and becomes mobile, you can add play-group to your busy list, and over the years you can add ballet, piano, footy, Mandarin lessons, yoga, karate, extra tuition (to make up for the fact that your kids are falling behind in reading because they're spending all their time doing extracurricular activities instead of reading a book), T-ball, tennis, cricket, musical theatre and chess.

Think back to your own childhood. What did you do after school? I'll bet it didn't involve being ferried from pillar to post.

Modern parents need to collectively calm the fuck down.

BUSY PARENTING

I put the following questions to parents from all over the country:

Do you think that there is a link between childhood anxiety and over-programmed children?
Do your kids have an organised activity on most afternoons?
What do your kids do after school?

My kids are too little for all that, but as a former teacher, I like to remember that all children need down time and even boredom. Boredom stimulates creativity; over-programming does the opposite. It stifles creativity. Creativity is important if children are to learn to think 'outside the box', to come up with new solutions and to develop self-confidence.

I absolutely think there is a link. I firmly believe my kids need down time to just be kids and play. Currently my kids have no organised activities (aside from weekend swimming lessons) as I felt like the start of the school year needed their full attention. I plan to let them start something now that we are into second term. After school, my kids play . . . that's it.

I try to keep weekday afternoons free for home-work and relaxing. Friday nights we have footy, Saturday morning swimming lessons. That's enough for us.

My two boys, ages ten and six, do homework after school, swimming on Saturdays and Nippers on Sundays in summer. We can have our own fun without it being an organised activity.

We underestimate the value of unstructured play . . . It's when children learn how to deal with conflict, and about cooperation, turn-taking and fair play.

My kids play one sport (soccer) and do one social activity (guides/scouts). That's it. So that's two afternoons a week; the other three weekday afternoons we are all at home. Any more than that that would definitely lead to anxiety; as it is, my highly strung daughter worries that she won't get all her home-work done.

If children love what they're doing, then I can't see how after-school activities would make them anxious, but if they're not really invested and it's more the parents who want them to do it then, yes, it could very well be making them anxious. My six-year-old does ballet one night a week and my ten-year-old does ballet one night and tap another night. Two nights of activities is enough and she knows that if she wants to do something else, then either ballet or tap has to go.

My eight-year-old has netball training one afternoon, a game on Saturday morning, and has piano lessons one afternoon plus fifteen minutes' practice every morning before school. My six-year-old has scouts one afternoon a week and an activity one weekend a month. Perfect for us, not too much running around and more than enough 'free days' for non-organised stuff.

As children's freedom has declined, so has their creativity, it seems.

Child behaviourist and all-round legend Nathalie Brown has this to say about the over-programmed child:

After twenty years' experience, one pattern I have really noticed—and it saddens me to say that it's on the rise—is that children as young as four are showing signs of stress: stress that is debilitating in exactly the same way as it is for us grown-ups. The stress the children are demonstrating is showing up and reflected in their behaviour, such as being exhausted at school, being overemotional, having meltdowns and general 'misbehaviour'. Of course you have to take into account a child's individuality—while one child may cope really well with four after-school activities a week, not all will. Some children are not coping with having so much on their plate. Too often I hear:

'I'd like to make an appointment for you to see my six-year-old daughter.'

'Sure. How about next Wednesday at 4 pm?'

'Oh, we can't do Wednesday—she's swimming.'

'What about Thursday?'

'Thursday she does gymnastics, Monday she has keyboard and dance, and on Tuesdays and Saturdays she does netball.'

I feel for both the child and the parent who is ferrying this child around.

Observing children is a major part of what I do; I watch them at school and at their after-school activities. I am all for children having interests, participating in competitions, learning through play, but not to the level where it becomes detrimental to the child. Waking your child at 5.30 am for a relaxing and mindful yoga lesson five times a week before school only to have them dozing at their desk by 10 am is somewhat missing the point of the mindful yoga class.

If you can picture how well a child keeps it together at school for over six hours in a structured environment, which I find incredible, plus homework, they will also need unstructured time to just be. To just be a child.

We all have dreams for our children, we all want the best for them, we want them to have opportunities to flourish, but it is crucial to remember the child too, that their dreams are not our dreams and not every waking moment has to be filled with something for them to do.

Amen, Nathalie! *fist bump and a high five for common sense!*

So I must ask the question: Why do we wear our busy-ness like it is a badge of honour?

I grew up in an era where there was no homework. You had your little reader in the early years, but afternoons were spent playing. Playing with your siblings and neighbours. The word 'play date' wasn't even a thing.

I try to keep it simple with my kids. They have boundaries, and it is up to them what they do within those boundaries to keep themselves amused. They have to be home by 5 pm. If they end up at a mate's house, they know to make a quick call home to let me know where they are. They are free to roam the streets on their bikes and explore the bushlands that surround our suburb. They know my phone number by heart and are well versed when it comes to stranger danger.

I believe that by giving kids their freedom—at the appropriate time, obviously—you are handing them the keys to so many of life's lessons that are more important than playing the oboe. They will learn to take risks and experience the consequences of their actions. This is important when learning about decision-making.

My good pal Mrs Goodman and I quite often discuss this topic. She once told me: 'Life is always going to knock it out of you, so you'd better start with a full tank.'

Never a truer word was spoken. You start at 100 per cent, and as you get older you take the knocks. How much those knocks diminish you is in your hands. I believe in teaching your kids confidence while they are under your roof, because once they are gone, they have to deal with the knocks on their own.

One afternoon, I saw Harry wheeling his bike down the driveway, his backpack on his back.

'Where are you going?' I asked him.

Without missing a beat, he looked at me and said, 'Wherever the wind takes me.'

It turns out he was off to the house around the corner for a dip in their pool . . . but good answer!

—31—

SCHOOL EXCURSIONS

When my son was in Year 6, he brought home a note from school that, naturally, I found in his bag covered in leftover lunchbox contents.

'What is this?' I asked him.

He shrugged. 'I dunno. Something about a school excursion.'

I read the note and then fell to the floor in a dead faint. I was expecting something about the zoo, or the Opera House. But no. The school excursion was to South Korea. Apparently my kids' school has a sister school there, so someone came up with the great idea of popping on over to say g'day.

When I'd regained consciousness, I gently broke the news to my son that he had as much chance of going to South Korea as I had of winning Mr Trump's Miss Universe competition. He asked me what my chances of winning such a competition were and I told him. Zero. He protested for a bit, listing for me which of his friends' parents were happy to fork out upwards of $3000 for this 'culturally rich' experience, but I shut the whole conversation down in a mature fashion by simply leaving the room.

It is probably worth noting that my kids did not go to an expensive private school where trips to Paris are the norm, but to the local primary school down the end of the road.

While I look back on my own school excursions fondly, they could be decidedly bizarre. One time, when I was a slogging through a course called Maths in Society (commonly called Maths in Space because it was for those of us who were having trouble counting up to one hundred), we were told that we were going on a very special excursion—a maths excursion!

And where do you go on a maths excursion?

McDonald's!

The educational objective of the excursion was to study the tessellations on the tiles in the restaurant. Hey, that was fine by me! All of a sudden we were the envy of our brainier peers; it turned out there was a silver lining to being dumb.

So the seven students of Maths in Society and our teacher, Mrs Prescott, went along to the nearest McDonald's and looked at tiles before chowing down on cheeseburgers and fries. I do believe that was the best day at school I ever had.

One of the things we really got stuck into when I was in primary school was good old-fashioned Australian history, which now goes by the rather more glamorous moniker of Human Society and Its Environment. (That is what HSIE stands for, if you have ever wondered.) An excursion was arranged to Old Sydney Town (now defunct, as there were no longer enough bums on seats to make it a viable concern).

Old Sydney Town was about a three-hour bus ride away. From memory, it was a collection of ye olde buildings, including a kiosk at which you could buy a carton of Ribena or a packet of Toobs from a busty wench.

It seemed that everyone who lived back in the olden days was either a soldier or a convict. We watched as a crime was committed, followed by a chase scene and an arrest. A court-room drama was acted out, and the punishment delivered. A flogging!

The criminal was tied up with his hands above his head while some sadist went to town on his back with a cat-o'-nine tails. I had my eyes closed and my hands squished firmly into my ears the entire time.

When finally the crowd's lust for gore was satisfied, it was revealed that the deep red welts on the criminal's back were in fact caused by food dye that had been liberally applied to the whip. And the bloke had not been writhing in real pain but was, it turned out, a mighty fine actor, whom we later saw smoking a cigarette and chatting to his erstwhile tormentor.

After watching a lady make a candle from beeswax and another lady spin some wool, we were hustled back on the bus for home. I cannot recall it being a fantastic excursion, but it sure beat the time we went to see a sewage plant . . .

✷

I will never forget the excitement I would feel when my teacher announced to the class that we were going on an excursion. A day off school! YES! But these days, the fun of an excursion comes with a little something called a risk management plan, in which any potential risk must be identified and assessed.

But while I might roll my eyes at this prim expression of pessimism, it does occur to me that educational authorities might have good reason to make these plans mandatory.

There was no risk management in 1991 when I, along with the rest of the Year 12 art class, boarded a bus and travelled eight hours and forty-three minutes from Sydney to Melbourne to visit some art galleries. Though, being seventeen, we were less interested in art than we were in shaking off the teachers and painting the town red.

So after a day of looking at art, we had dinner with the teachers and demurely bade them goodnight. (They were no doubt desperate to get rid of us so they could get stuck into the gin.) But what they didn't know was that we had a cunning plan that involved one of Melbourne's famed nightclubs, which happened to be not far from our digs.

It was like a whole new world. The music was completely doof-doof and I knew none of it. What was wrong with Color Me Badd? Cher? Heavy D & the Boyz? Nuh. This edgy Melbourne nightclub was having none of that. This was house music. And I was not a fan.

I sat with my friends, sucking back on a Sub Zero (with grenadine because I was at a funky Melbourne nightclub, trying to be cool), while men approached and tried to crack on to the prettier girls in our group, little realising that we were all under eighteen.

But that was no problem. We were all in possession of a folded, creased, dirty piece of paper created to assure the authorities that we were of legal drinking age.

Did I say 'created'? I did.

So, either you bribed your older sister to photocopy her driver's licence for you or, if your older sister was a bitch face from hell and refused, you did it the hard way. You photocopied your birth certificate and typed up a new birthdate on a fresh piece of paper, then, with the steady hand of the brain surgeon you were not destined to become, you carefully cut out the new date and pasted it over the original date on your birth certificate. After a few minutes' drying time, you photocopied the result. Then you studied the photocopy. Were there any shadows? Was the new date perfectly aligned? Yes? Then let's get back to that nightclub . . .

After a while, those Sub Zeros kicked in and, all of a sudden, I fucking loved house music! The lights and music throbbed through my veins as I spun around that dance floor, bumping into people and doing some exceptional interpretive dance with complete strangers. I spied a few of our posse doing shots of tequila at the bar. The night wore on, and our group of bright-eyed and bushy-tailed teenagers became less bright-eyed and less bushy-tailed.

And then I saw something so outrageous that I immediately raced over to the bar and screamed: 'Kirsty Owen is PASHING A GIRL!'

Kirsty was one of my friends. She was very cool, exceedingly beautiful and now, apparently, gay. We watched her suck face for an eternity on that dance floor. Was this a cool thing? Was this what you did in Melbourne?

After a while, Kirsty came up for air and I realised that she had not been pashing a girl, but pashing a beautiful man with long flowing locks. Long flowing locks on a man was not something that you saw every day on the streets of the conservative North Shore in Sydney. The fact that she'd pashed a man with long hair just made Kirsty even cooler in my eyes. Long hair! Who would have thought it?

The sun was starting to pop its head up to say hello, so we bade farewell to all our new mates and headed back to the hotel. Many of us lost our guts on the way back, and by the time our heads hit the pillows, sleep came very easy to us all.

About an hour later, our teacher banged on the door, reminding us to get our shit sorted because we had to be on the bus in twenty minutes. When no one replied, she opened the door, to be greeted with a great big pongy waft of tequila.

You could tell by her face that she knew what we had been up to, and that she was aware that if anyone found out we'd wandered the streets of Melbourne hideously drunk while on her watch, she was screwed.

So she did what any teacher would do in this situation. She said nothing. And up until now, none of us ever divulged the truth of that evening. If there were such a thing as a risk management plan back then, it would be worth no more than the paper it was printed on.

ARE WE THERE YET?

No more pencils, no more books . . .
No more teacher's dirty looks.

Let's face it, when you're a kid, the best part of the school year is the holidays. When I was growing up, our school year was divided up into three terms. When you consider how stuffed, emotional and cranky kids can be at the end of nine weeks, can you begin to imagine what they'd be like if they were schooled for fourteen weeks without a break? The situation would be DIRE. And those poor teachers . . . No wonder the four-term model was welcomed with open arms.

For me, school holidays were heaven. My siblings and I were mainly left to our own devices, but the best thing—the best thing *ever*—was going to our grandparents' farm in the country. We would all squish into Mum's Mazda RZ7 and take the Putty Road through the Yengo National Park, stopping at Mellong for a wee (and, more often than not, an enormous spew) before continuing on the windy road to Singleton. From there it it was on to Aberdeen and then Scone. Once you reached Scone you had a sniff of hope that you might actually one day reach your destination. It was also the point at which we would begin the time-honoured chant: 'Are we there yet?'

After what seemed like eleven years, the farms would start to thin out and big signs would appear, alerting us to the fact that we were about to reach the Country Music Capital of our fair nation. The atmosphere in the car underwent a shift from frustration to anticipation.

Tamworth: the city of my conception and birth. A town not unlike Paris in that it, too, is divided by a mighty river (in this case the Peel) and was known at one time as the City of Lights, by virtue of the fact that it was the first place in Australia to have electric streetlights installed.

We would often drive down Callala Lane to look at the house where I spent the first few years of my life. Every year, it seemed smaller than it had the year before. And then we'd be leaving Tamworth behind, and farming land once again took over the landscape. We were headed for the tiny hamlet of Kootingal. Kootingal was everything a small country town should be: it had a smattering of houses, a school, a pub, a town hall, the cop shop and, of course, the bowling club.

Nanna and Poppa lived on a couple of acres. As we cruised up the driveway, they'd appear on the front verandah. After hugs and kisses, we'd always rush straight to the kitchen to be measured. The back of the kitchen door told the story of our growth. There would be minor celebrations over how much we had shot up since our last visit. And with that formality over, the rest of our stay would be devoted purely to pleasure.

Poppa was famous for breeding the most slow and docile racehorses in the district, so we had access to transport. One particular day, we packed up some sandwiches and decided to go further than we had ever been before—that is, to the far corner of the farm, where there was allegedly an abandoned piggery. My sister and I were double dinking on a big horse called Bull (his real name was Bullshit, but Poppa called him Bull in front of us), and our brother walked alongside, accompanied by Poppa's Australian Silky Terriers, Bacardi and Coke.

Up and over the hills we went, avoiding the rabbit holes and keeping an eye out for friends of the slithering type. The sun beat down and turned our shoulders and noses red, but we were determined to reach this mythical piggery. At long last, we crested a hill and there it sat behind a barbed-wire fence.

We slid off Bull's back and tethered him to a tree before slowly and carefully climbing through the barbed wire. The place was an absolute dive, so naturally we loved it. We ate our picnic on a fallen tree before exploring the old buildings. And in one of these buildings we discovered a stack of pig carcasses and bones.

We stood, horrified, staring at this grisly scene. Then my sister shouted: 'Quick! Run! This place is HAUNTED!'

Now, my sister is a champion over-reactor, so usually I took her warnings with a grain of salt, but she was so convincing on this occasion that I made a mad dash for the barbed-wire fence.

Of course, the one thing every kid learns about successfully negotiating barbed wire is that it takes time and patience. But when the ghosts of a dozen zombie skeleton pigs are chasing you, time is not your friend! We shredded ourselves stupid in our haste to escape their evil trotters.

Adrenalin pumping, my sister and I leapt onto Bull and bolted up the hill, leaving our brother and Bacardi and Coke to scurry along behind us. When we arrived back at the house, we breathlessly recounted our adventure to Nanna as she bathed our punctured skin with red Mercurochrome.

The red Mercurochrome was never far from hand during our visits to the farm. I recall one time Poppa got out the little quad bike to teach us how to ride. The front yard was the size of a football field and in the dead centre sat a huge cactus—into which I promptly steered that bike.

I still carry a massive scar on my shin from that episode. If Poppa hadn't been so stuck into his KB, perhaps a trip to emergency might have been more effective than a tousle of my hair and a 'She'll be right'.

It is a very deep scar.

I loved our holidays at Kootingal. I loved being shown how to load up the slug gun and shoot Nanna's empty TAB cans off the back gate. I loved visiting the neighbours and swimming in their pool. I loved eating Nanna's food. One time, as we were leaving for home, she snuck my sister and I each a bottle of our favourite cordial for the trip. My favourite was raspberry and my sister's was lime. I cannot recall my brother being there, but trust me, if he had been, I wouldn't have forgotten . . .

For halfway down the Putty Road, I started vomiting up copious amounts of red liquid. Mum pulled the car over just as my sister started hurling great quantities of green spew all over herself. Had my brother been there, I'm pretty sure he would have added orange to the mix.

✳

Holidays at home were a different kind of adventure. One treat was to go to the movies at the Regent in Richmond. This was the real deal—none of this megaplex crap. The Regent was a proper cinema with one lady sitting in a tiny booth selling tickets and another lady sitting in a tiny booth selling lollies.

Once you'd bought your Maltesers you'd choose whether to sit upstairs or downstairs. We always chose upstairs, as there were always rowdy children *shifts eyes* who would take great pleasure in throwing things from the top level down onto the unsuspecting audience below.

Just before the feature film came on, the manager of the cinema would get up on stage and tell us about the movies that were going to be screened in the coming months. It was a little bit like watching trailers, I suppose. Then the lights would dim and the lion would roar, signalling that it was time for the food fight to commence!

Another regular holiday activity would be a day spent at the Skatel. The Skatel was a really rundown skating rink next to the railway tracks. Mum would be drop us off there in the morning and pick us up in the early evening. Skate hire was included in the entrance fee. The skates on offer were dog-poo brown with orange laces and I was always jealous of those girls who swanned about in those white leather boots with sparkly red wheels.

Mainly, though, we spent our holidays mooching around the neighbourhood, playing with other kids.

School holidays these days look completely different. Somehow we've fallen into the trap of thinking that if our kids are not spending every waking second doing something enriching and educational, then we are failing them as parents.

But this could not be further from the truth. We need to allow our kids to explore. Both anxiety and obesity are on the rise, and I can't help but believe it is linked to the passive lifestyle a lot of kids live these days, spending hours and hours watching crap on screens accompanied by constant snacking on crap.

They say knowledge is power and mostly I agree. But I also think that, to a certain degree, knowledge can lead to fear. Our generation is obsessed with the details, the dangers. Is it organic? Is it safe? What are the standards and are they being met?

We teach our children to be suspicious, to be guarded, to be worried.

Ask yourself: would you let your three young kids ride big horses bareback over dusty fields, dodging snakes, shredding themselves on wire and getting chased by zombie ghost pigs?

Would you drop them off for the day at a dodgy skating rink with nothing but three bucks in their pocket for the day? No mobile emergency contact form to fill in. No indemnity to sign. (And there's a DJ in the music booth who likes to take photos of all the kids.)

Well?

School holidays are slow and fast. They are boring and hectic. They are fun and infuriating. As a child you cannot wait for them to start, and as a parent you cannot wait for them to finish.

School days are also slow and fast and boring and hectic. At the time, when you are a kid, time kind of stands still when you are at school. Lessons are long, distractions are everywhere. When you are a teacher, it is pretty much the same.

And then you have babies. In the blink of an eye they are starting school. What happened? How did that time go by so fast? But it doesn't stop, and year in and year out they grow and change and learn and throw immense challenges at you. You navigate the maze that is their educational journey with triumphs, and a few tears.

'Are we there yet?' is often asked a thousand times on long, hot, uncomfortable car rides and it is also what we, as parents, tend to say at the end of each school holidays. But the truth is that these school years are fleeting and, as evident in these very pages, can leave so many memories that stay with you, well past the final bell.

ACKNOWLEDGEMENTS

To the supreme team at Allen & Unwin, my unreserved thanks. Publisher Jane Palfreyman took a punt on a mouthy housewife and made this book happen. Christa Munns, uber editor, helped knock it all together, and big thanks to Ali Lavau for all her great work and encouragement. A group hug goes out to all the primary school teachers out there—you do amazing work.

Parts of this book contain stories from my community of WoogsWorld readers, and I would like to thank them for not only these anecdotes, but for their wonderful support over the years. And may I mention Shae Reynolds, Kirsten Smith and Emily Toxward, who generously contributed to *Primary School Confidential*. I thank you.

And to my beloved Mr Woog: see, I told you I could finish it!